The Genesis of the State

The GENESIS of the STATE

MARTIN SICKER

PRAEGER

New York
Westport, Connecticut
London

Library of Congress Cataloging-in-Publication Data

Sicker, Martin.
    The genesis of the state / Martin Sicker.
        p.   cm
    Includes bibliographical references and index.
    ISBN 0–275–93704–6
    1. State, The—Origin. 2. Authority.   I. Title.
GN492.6.S53   1991
320.1—dc20   90–7375

British Library Cataloguing-in-Publication Data is available.

Library of Congress Catalog Card Number: 90–7375
ISBN: 0–275–93704–6

First published in 1991

Praeger Publishers, One Madison Avenue, New York, NY 10010
An imprint of Greenwood Publishing Group, Inc.

Printed in the United States of America

∞

The paper used in this book complies with the
Permanent Paper Standard issued by the National
Information Standards Organization (Z39.48–1984).

10 9 8 7 6 5 4 3 2 1

Contents

Introduction

As in so many fields of human endeavor, intellectual as well as practical, the study of political thought, too, is affected by fads and fashions. Particularly as contemporary political scientists strive to raise their field to the level of a true human science, seeking to evolve theories and, prospectively, even laws of political behavior analogous to those found in the natural sciences, certain topics of classical political philosophy have become unfashionable.

One of the subjects that has lost interest for many if not most contemporary scholars and students of politics is the theory of the state. Indeed, at one point in recent memory there was a tendency of some writers to try and do away with the term itself as a descriptor of a particular political phenomenon, as though getting rid of the word would also eliminate the profound problems with which the theory of the state attempts to grapple.

This attitude is quite baffling since the existence of the state is a reality of everyday life and experience. In fact, our daily newspapers remind us of this constantly as they attempt to inform the public about those issues that impact on our lives. What literate person has not been exposed, to one degree or another, to the numerous contentious questions that are raised continually about the separation of church and state? Whether it is a matter of prayer in the public schools, the teaching of evolution or creationism as science, or governmental funding of textbooks in parochial schools, the issue always reduces to whether there is an overriding "state interest" that justifies governmental action or inaction, depending on circumstances. Similarly, one of the most controversial issues confronting government and the public in the United States today, the question of the public funding of abortions, is defined in terms of whether there is a compelling "state interest" for the national and state governments to take a position on the matter one way or another.

Notwithstanding the frequency and commonality of its use, the notion of the state remains one that is not generally well understood, even though it is an intrinsic component of our political vocabulary. It is therefore surprising that more attention has not been paid to explicating and clarifying the conception of the state. The idea for this small book on the state arose from a series of informal discussions on political questions that the author conducted several years ago with a number of friends, professionals and scholars in other fields, who were interested in gaining some greater insight into the fundamental nature of some of the political phenomena and events that affected their lives as individuals and as citizens.

The issues that come under the study of "the state" are considerable, and this short work is concerned only with one aspect, albeit an important one, of the broader subject. The primary focus here is on the basic question of the genesis of the state and political authority. How did the state originate and what is the source of its authority? This is far more than a merely academic question. The fundamental political question regarding the moral obligation of a citizen to obey the state is intimately related to the issue of the legitimacy of the state's authority, and the latter depends in large measure on its sources. Accordingly, one's position on the matter of political obligation will depend to some extent on the theory of the origin of the state that one accepts as valid. This present work will examine the several major approaches to the question of the genesis of the state and political authority that are reflected in the works of a wide range of philosophers and thinkers throughout the ages, and will conclude by suggesting what might constitute a serviceable contemporary answer.

The question of the origin of the state is one that has been of concern to people throughout the world and, in this work, an attempt will be made to examine some expressions of that concern from non-Western sources as well as from the mainstreams of Western political culture. Unfortunately, the study of non-Western political thought is still at such a rudimentary stage that there is a great paucity of relevant studies and information regarding the many diverse political cultures that reflect the heritages of the vast majority of the world's population. As a consequence, the use of such material here is limited to that small amount readily accessible to the author. Moreover, since the primary concern here is with the formulation of the diverse notions of the state and its origins rather than with the exposition of the complete theory of the state of any particular political philosopher or theorist, the works of such writers will be broached only to the extent that they bear on the specific issue under consideration. This latter approach may elicit the criticism that it does an injustice to the thought of such theorists and is in effect quoting them out of context. I have tried to avoid citing authors in a way that may be misleading with regard to their ultimate positions on fundamental political questions. However, it must be recognized that the works cited herein are drawn on only for the purpose of illustrating the diverse formulations of the theories of the genesis of the state for their current relevance and not for the purpose of assessing a particular writer's full perspective on the nature of the state. Thus it will be found that writers who may have similar views with regard to the genesis of the state may hold radically different positions with regard to the implications of that theory of origins. In other words, in this work, I am less concerned with what a particular writer intended than with what his actual statement conveys to us in the present, and thereby helps us think about the issue under discussion.

Finally, the book essentially discounts the conventional notion, common in the literature of political theory, which treats the several theoretical formulations of the origin of the state as overlapping stages in the development of political theory. As will be seen, there is little real basis for the latter approach. While it is a commonplace assumption that social contract theory supplanted patriarchal theory, and was itself disposed of by the arguments of David Hume, the fact is that both theories have survived into the twentieth century and that although social contract theory may be in disfavor in academic circles, its tenets are nonetheless reflected in much of the discussion that actually takes place in the political and policy-making arenas. Similarly, the divine theory, the force theory, and the organic theory of the state are all still thriving both in the Western and non-Western worlds, in political practice if not in the academy. As suggested earlier, it is still too early, because of the absence of sufficient accessible materials from the non-western world, to write a comprehensive history of the theories of the genesis of the state. In this regard, this book may serve as a preliminary outline of such a project.

The volume opens with a brief discussion of the definition of the state, so as to establish a reasonable common ground for considering the several primary approaches to the theory of the genesis of the state and political authority that are presented in the subsequent chapters. It is the author's hope that this book will help the reader gain some further insight into and appreciation for the universal concern throughout history regarding the true nature of the state and the basis for its intrusion, beneficent or malevolent, into the life of the individual, the family, and the society.

*The Genesis
of the State*

1

What Is the State?

It has been the common experience of humankind throughout recorded history, from remote antiquity to the present and in every part of the globe, to band together in associations for a variety of general or specific purposes. Typically, these associations have been concerned with the common physical, spiritual, social, and economic interests of their members. How is this fact, that man is everywhere to be found as a member of one or more such associations, to be explained? Is it because man is a social creature by his very nature and therefore instinctively forms associations with others of his species? If this is the case, as is argued by some, the small number of hermits that have appeared throughout the ages would properly be seen as aberrations from the normal and natural. On the other hand, some others will suggest that man's sociability, above and beyond his natural tendency to mate and form familial associations, is a reflection of his basic inability to cope without external assistance with the challenges he must confront from the environments, natural or man-made, within which he must function. However, this latter view implies that if man were capable of adequately dealing with the vicissitudes of his environment without the cooperation of others, there would seem to be no compelling need or purpose for such extrafamilial associations.

Seen from this latter perspective, man's attempts to meet his individual needs, as well as those of family members immediately dependent upon him, are constrained by the significant limitations imposed by nature on the individual's ability to achieve these ends by himself. It therefore seems reasonable to assume that a variety of human associations were—and—are formed because of such unsatisfied individual needs that cannot be fulfilled by solitary persons. These unsatisfied needs may result from deficiencies intrinsic to the individual. A person may simply be physically unable to carry out certain activities without the assistance of other people. To remedy this situation he may enter into a cooperative association with others for the purpose of a collaborative effort to achieve goals that are foreclosed to the individual. An argument in favor of this perception is reflected in the works of Plato. At one point he has Socrates say: "A State, I said, arises, as I conceive, out of the needs of mankind; no one is self-sufficing, but all of us have many wants. . . . Then, as we have many wants, and many persons are needed to supply them, one takes a helper for one purpose and another for another; and when these partners and helpers are gathered together in one habitation the body of inhabitants is termed a State."[1] Although Plato evidently makes the case that societies arise out of the need for economic cooperation, suggesting the need for some sort of consensual agreement to bring the city into being, it is an issue of on-going scholarly debate as to whether such is a proper interpretation of his intention in these passages.[2]

On the other hand, man's unsatisfied needs may be primarily the direct consequence of certain deficiencies in the environment, deficiencies that may be summarized in a single word: scarcity. Scarcity may be the most significant characteristic of virtually all societies, not necessarily in any absolute sense but certainly in light of the expectations and wishes of their members. In other words, the demand for the bounties of the environment may and most often do exceed the available supply. Scarcity, whether of physical goods such as shelter, food and water, and sexual partners, or of less tangible psychological goods such as satisfaction, esteem, and other forms of personal gratification, gives these goods special value. Because they are in limited supply, competition for them creates tensions and conflicts over their acquisition and retention. This too has been the common experience of mankind. Consequently, one of the primary tasks of human associations, and a principal reason for their formation in the first place, is to deal with the problem of how to allocate these scarce goods among their members and thereby prevent or reduce the level of violence resulting from competition for such goods.

This problem has been resolved in a variety of ways within the different kinds of human associations that are known to have existed. In some primitive societies, but not very many, the competition for the scarce is virtually eliminated or at least significantly reduced through the adoption of a societal regime of individual self-denial and communal sharing, in effect, adjusting the demand to equal the available supply. However, as desirable as such an unselfish approach to dealing with the problems of scarcity may appear to be, it is not reflective of the general experience of societies that is revealed on the bloody pages of human history. Accordingly, David Easton, who analyzed society in systemic terms, observed: "In every society, there is a variety of means for regulating or resolving differences with regard to the way in which scarce values are to be distributed and used. But where such differences cannot be adjusted privately, that is, autonomously, among the members of the society, or where the achievement of a goal requires mobilization of the resources and energies of all members of a system, resort to some sort of political allocation becomes inevitable."[3]

When a particular human association does not rely on the voluntary self-denial of the competitors for the scarce goods of value that come within its sphere of concern, but makes the allocation of those values to its members authoritatively, that is, where it makes a determination on behalf of the society as a whole as to how, under what conditions, and to whom to award the scarce goods that are available, and when the relevant allocative decisions are vested in a central determinative body within the broader association, the latter is considered to have assumed a political form and a state is said to have come into existence. For Easton, a political system is defined essentially in terms of its processes for the authoritative allocation of values for a society. "All political systems as such are distinguished by the fact that if we are to be able to describe them as persisting, we must attribute to them the successful fulfillment of two functions. They must be able to allocate values for a society; they must also manage to induce most members to accept these allocations as binding, at least most of the time. . . . These two distinctive features—the allocation of values for a society and the relative frequency of compliance with them—are the essential variables of political life."[4]

Dealing with the issue from a related although somewhat different sociological perspective, Franz Oppenheimer suggested that there are two inherently opposed approaches through which man can obtain those objects of value to satisfy his needs and wants. One approach is economic, by which man expends his energies to achieve his ends, that is, he works for them. The other approach is political, or what Oppenheimer terms, "the forcible appropriation of the labor of others." In his view, the institutionalization within society of this latter approach to resolving the allocation problem constitutes the state. Oppenheimer writes: "No state, therefore, can come into being until the economic means has created a definite number of objects for the satisfaction of needs, which objects may be taken away or appropriated. . . . For that reason, primitive huntsmen are without a state; and even the more highly developed huntsmen become parts of a state structure only when they find in their neighborhood an evolved economic organization which they can subjugate."[5]

A substantially different approach to understanding the genesis of the state was set forth by Carl Schmitt, who saw its origin in the inherent need of the political society for security from threats to its existence. Starting with the proposition that "the concept of the state presupposes the concept of the political,"[6] Schmitt argues that one can arrive at a useful definition of the "political" only by discovering what distinctive categories of ideas and activities come under such a rubric. In this regard, he insists that "the political has its own criteria which express themselves in a characteristic way. The political must therefore rest on its own ultimate distinctions, to which all action with a specifically political meaning can be traced." Examining other categories of human thought and action, Schmitt suggests that each has its distinctive focus: aesthetics is concerned with the criteria of the beautiful and the ugly; economics deals with the profitable and the unprofitable; morality is concerned with the ultimate distinctions between good and evil. The question he raises is whether the political also has such a delimiting criterion that makes the ideas and activity that it encompasses equally distinctive. For the category of the political to be meaningful it must deal with fundamental distinctions that are not the subject of any other discipline. For Schmitt, "the specific political distinction to which political actions and motives can be reduced is that between friend and enemy."[7] In his view, then, the essential value that must be assured politically is the societal value of security.

Although Schmitt's primary concern is with external threats to the society, the essential applicability of his position to internal threats as well is reflected in the more recent work of Leslie Lipson. Starting from the commonsense proposition that security of life and limb is one of the common concerns of all people, Lipson suggests that men everywhere seek assurances of protection from physical harm. Although this imperative of security is universal, different societies have employed varying means of providing for it. Thus, it is by no means uncommon to find people relying primarily upon themselves for the security they crave, an approach exemplified in the notion of the rugged, self-sufficient individual. However, as Lipson points out, self-reliance was not always an adequate response to the threat of harm. "This was especially so when the likelihood of attack was constant, rather than intermittent; when the techniques available to an aggressor placed the defense at a disadvantage; and when the chief disturbance to one's peace came, not from within the group, but from the organized strength of another group outside. Effective security, therefore, had to be collective security." Under such circumstances men had little option other than to find means of cooperating as a group in a common defense effort. Lipson then goes on to argue that once a group need such as protection becomes a constant, the methods and processes through which the group meets that need tend to be repeated, presumably because if they work there is no reason to change them. By consistent repetition and application, these measures gain group-wide acknowledgment and acceptance as the appropriate means for satisfying a basic societal need. "They are then endowed with formal organization. In a word, they are institutionalized. What we call an 'institution' is the outgrowth in organized form of the repetitive practices with which a group fulfills a common need. The state originates, in short, when a group of persons have institutionalized their own protection."[8]

The approaches of both Easton and Oppenheimer, which are based on the presumption of unsatisfied needs and wishes resulting from scarcity as the motivating factor for the formation of the state, and those of Schmitt and Lipson, which are predicated on the conviction that the fundamental motivating factor is physical insecurity, may appear to be incompatible. However, upon reflection, it seems clear that the latter approaches may be subsumed under the former, which are more comprehensive. Thus, the imperatives of individual and collective security, and the existence of credible threats thereto, may be considered in Easton's terms as but additional scarce, albeit critical, values that can be relatively satisfied only through the formation of the state and its assumption of an authoritative allocative role for the society. Indeed, such a fusion of these considerations was postulated during the medieval period by Marsilius of Padua. He argued that since individual man comes into the world essentially defenseless against his external environment, "he needed arts of diverse genera and species to avoid the aforementioned harms. But since these arts can be exercised only by a large number of men, and can be had only through their association with one another, men had to assemble together in order to attain what was beneficial through these arts and to avoid what was harmful." However, Marsilius also considered it inevitable that disagreements would arise among the members of the community which would lead to conflicts that, if left unchecked, would precipitate its ultimate destruction. Consequently, "there had to be established in this association a standard of justice and a guardian . . . to restrain excessive wrongdoers as well as other individuals both within and outside the state who disturb or attempt to oppress the community." Therefore, Marsilius concluded, "men, then, were assembled for the sake of the sufficient life, being able to seek out for themselves the necessaries enumerated above, and exchanging them with one to another. This assemblage, thus perfect and having the limit of self-sufficiency, is called the state."[9]

Notwithstanding the preceding discussion, we are still without a clear statement of precisely what is intended to be conveyed by use of the term "state." Indeed, one of the recurring problems in the literature of political theory is the formulation of an adequate definition of the term. Unfortunately, many of the definitions proposed over the last century, while by no means incorrect, are nevertheless too broad or too vague to be of much value as a guide to the appropriate use of the term. Thus, according to Heinrich von Treitschke, "The State is the people, legally united as an independent entity."[10] A somewhat more serviceable notion of the state was postulated as a generalized proposition by Westel W. Willoughby: "Wherever there can be discovered in any community of men a supreme authority exercising a control over the social actions of individuals and groups of individuals, and itself subject to no such regulation, there we have a State."[11] This idea was recast by Robert Paul Wolff into the concise definition: "The state is a group of persons who have and exercise supreme authority within a given territory."[12]

By contrast, Agost Pulszky went considerably further than the preceding definitions with the following assertion: "That

moment of the organization of every society in which it presents itself as independent, dominant, and capable of asserting its own conditions of life by force, forms always a
distinct phase in the process of association; and whenever
any particular society assumes this form it appears as the
State. The State is properly a law-creating and law-main-
taining society which proclaims and asserts the conditions of
its existence in connection with its own conduct and that of
its subjects, through commanding, permissive, and prohi-
bitory rules."[13] Pulszky's introduction of the element of force
into the definition of the state is particularly noteworthy.
There can be little doubt that the ability to mobilize and
apply force is a significant feature of the state throughout
history. Max Weber wrote in this regard: "Ultimately, one
can define the modern state sociologically only in terms of
the specific means peculiar to it, as to every political association, namely, the use of physical force.—Of course, force
is certainly not the normal or the only means of the state—
nobody says that—but force is a means specific to the state."[14]
More recently, Lipson observed that "many of the problems
which are peculiar to the state and distinguish it from other
human associations flow from the simple, but fundamental,
fact that the state must use force or it cannot even begin to
be a state."[15]

In his study of the medieval origins of the modern state,
Joseph R. Strayer also observes that most attempts at definition of a state have not proven very satisfactory. He then
suggests that a more useful approach might be to identify
some of the fundamental signs or criteria which indicate that
a state is in the process of coming into being. To constitute
the nucleus of a state, groups must first form a community
that persists over time and that is not just a temporary co-
alition formed to deal with some specific emergency. Second,
the community must undertake the development of permanent institutions that will serve to strengthen its political
cohesion and identity. Since it is difficult to establish permanent institutions where the territory over which they are
to operate changes continually, and where the physical cohesion of the group fluctuates in accordance with such changes,

a third criterion is geographical: The established community must encompass a stable core area, even though some variability in its outer limits may be acceptable. Fourth, the institutions of the community must be capable of surviving changes in leadership and fluctuations in the degree of cooperation that may exist among the community's component groups over time. Moreover, beyond demonstrating persistence, these political institutions must show signs of growing prestige and authority. Finally, and most importantly, Strayer asserts that there must be "a shift in loyalty from family, local community, or religious organization to the state and the acquisition by the state of a moral authority to back up its institutional structure and its theoretical legal supremacy. At the end of the process, subjects accept the idea that the interests of the state must prevail, that the preservation of the state is the highest social good."[16]

While Strayer's thesis is quite intriguing, his methodology may be subject to criticism. In essence, he is projecting backward from what is, or was known to exist, to determine what conditions had to be met in order to produce the modern state. However, it is conceivable that a similar result might have been produced by more than one set of factors. Consequently, it is by no means certain that the criteria that Strayer adduces are the only relevant ones. This leaves us, once again, in need of a serviceable definition of the state.

At the risk of producing yet another flawed definition, I would suggest the following as a tentative formulation that incorporates the essential elements that typify the state: The state is the corporate structure, coextensive with a political society, which is the locus of supreme political authority, and which can command an effective force monopoly to assure compliance with its decisions.

With the possible exception of some rare aboriginal societies that may still survive in the remote nooks and crannies of the earth, the state is unquestionably the ubiquitous form of societal governance in modern times. As a general rule, we find people everywhere regularly submitting to the control of a public authority that exercises its powers through an institutional arrangement designated as a government.

It is common practice among political theorists to draw a fundamental distinction between the state and the government. The government is, as Randolph Bourne wrote, "the machinery by which the nation, organized as a State, carries out its State functions. Government is a framework of the administration of laws, and the carrying out of the public force. Government is the idea of the State put into practical operation in the hands of definite, concrete, fallible men." However, although one can envisage the state only in the form of its government, it is an error to identify the two. "That the State is a mystical conception is something that must never be forgotten. Its glamor and its significance linger behind the framework of government and direct its activities."[17]

This differentiation of the government from the state, of which it is a manifestation, is significant because it facilitates consideration of the functional differences between the two concepts. Since the presumptive purpose of the government is to accomplish the aims of the state under a variety of circumstances and conditions, the form and character of any particular government becomes a matter of political expediency. Consequently, the removal or dissolution of a government does not necessarily imply the end of the state whose regime it constitutes. Under this conception, the state may continue to exist even as its instruments of rule rise and fall. Accordingly, it has been common in many societies to distinguish between the "head of state" and the "head of government." An example of this is the United Kingdom, where the queen serves as head of state, a position filled by the president in many republics, while the prime minister is the head of government. The value of the distinction may be seen in its practical effects. Thus, while the leadership of the government may change through the operation of the political process typical of a particular country, the head of state provides continuity that facilitates the transition from one regime to another. However, this is by no means a universal practice. In the United States, where the president is both head of state and head of government, the significance of the distinction between state and government seems rather questionable, and is often blurred.

Benedetto Croce, for one, took issue with those who would draw a sharp distinction between the two concepts. Accepting that "the word 'State' is meant to indicate all the institutions, customs and laws which govern the actions of man, and more precisely the whole body of fundamental and constitutional laws," Croce argued that it must be recognized that, in fact, laws are made by individual men within the context of the institution known as government. Therefore: "For those who seek concreteness rather than abstractions, the State is nothing but the government and assumes complete reality in the government; outside the unbroken chain of the actions of the government remain only the principle of the abstract necessity of these same actions and the assumption that the laws have an unchanging value of their own, different from the actions performed in their light or in their shadow."[18] In other words, Croce suggests that the essential difference between the state and government is that between an idea and its manifestation in reality. He would remind us that when we say that such and such are demands of the state, what we are really saying is that it is the individuals who are vested with political authority, who claim to embody the aims and purposes of the state, that are making these demands. The state itself, in this view, remains an abstraction, and as such cannot demand anything or take any concrete action. In this regard, it should be noted that the very term "state," derived from the Latin word *status*, which was first appropriated for the vocabulary of politics in the sixteenth century, originally referred to the standing or position within the political society of those who personified its authority.

Notwithstanding Croce's caveat, the distinction between a state and its government has proven useful in pointing out the differences between the relevant permanent and transitory aspects of political society, even if it might not stand the test of a rigorous empirical analysis. It should also be recognized that Croce's position itself entails some profound moral issues. Take, for example, the matter of capital punishment. If the state is acknowledged as a corporate being that is imposing sentence, those who carry it out effectively subsume their individual personalities under that of the state and act as its instruments. However, if the state is regarded as an abstraction that is incapable of taking action, the demand for capital punishment becomes merely that of individual men acting autonomously in the name of the state. Under such circumstances, what individual has the moral right to take it upon himself to take another's life? In other words, a criminal may justly be condemned to death, but who has the moral right to be his executioner, if in so acting he does not serve as an organ of a real state but merely as one individual killing another in the name of an abstraction. It does not help if one argues that he is acting as an instrument of the government, since the government itself is merely a group of men acting in the name of the state. If the government is more than that, then it too becomes an abstraction like the state and is incapable of making demands or taking action. It will be seen later that there is one school of political theorists who insist upon the reification of the state, transforming it from an abstraction into a living social organism.

In addition to the distinction between state and government, some writers also draw an additional distinction between the "idea" of the state and the "conception" of the state. Johann K. Bluntschli writes: "The conception (*Begriff*) of the State has to do with the nature and essential characteristics of actual States. The idea or ideal (*Idee*) of the State presents a picture, in the splendour of imaginary perfection, of the State as not yet realised, but to be striven for. The conception of the State can only be discovered by history; the idea of the State is called up by philosophical speculation."[19] This approach to the distinction between the idea and the concept of the state is amplified by John W. Burgess, who treated the two as existing in a more direct hierarchical relationship. Burgess states: "The idea of the state is the state perfect and complete. The concept of the state is the state developing and approaching perfection." The idea, he suggests, is "the pioneer of the concept, and the concept the stages in the realization of the idea." Burgess continues:

From the standpoint of the idea, the state is mankind viewed as an organized unit. From the standpoint of the concept, it is a particular portion of mankind viewed as an organized unit. From the standpoint of the idea the territorial basis of the State is the world, and the principle of unity is humanity. From the standpoint of the concept, again, the territorial basis of the state is a particular portion of the earth's surface, and the principle of unity is that particular phase of human nature, and of human need, which, at any particular stage in the development of that nature, is predominant and commanding. The former is the real state of the perfect future. The latter is the real state of the past, the present, and the imperfect future.[20]

This approach is sharply contested by Willoughby, who suggests that Burgess appears to be confusing states and governments. In his view, it is only governments, which constitute the machinery of the state, that can be characterized in terms of greater or lesser comparative excellence. He rejects Burgess's notion of the concept of the state as the state "approaching perfection," and insists that "there can be no such thing as an imperfect State."[21] Accordingly, Willoughby, who also distinguishes between the abstract idea of the state and the empiric concept of the state, takes a somewhat different approach to the matter. He asserts that "the first is what the Germans designate '*Staatsidee*,' being the idea of the State in its most general form. It is that idea which embraces all that is essential to, and which is possessed by all types of State life. It is the State reduced to its lowest terms. The empiric conception, on the other hand, is particular, and has reference to special civic types as historically manifested."[22] Thus, whereas Bluntschli and Burgess see the idea of the state as an intellectual model of perfection that real states attempt to emulate to one degree or another, Willoughby sees it more as an abstract generalization that reflects the essential characteristics of all states, but not as an idealized model that actual states seek to approximate.

As will be seen in the course of the chapters that follow,

while few political thinkers address the distinctions drawn here between the idea and the concept of the state, many do in fact seem to have an abstract model of the state in mind as they deliberate on the question of its genesis and the sources of its political authority. As a practical matter, no matter how organized, or in what manner their powers be exercised, all states serve substantially identical purposes and reflect a fundamental commonality in their intrinsic characters. One might suggest that the institutional make-up of the state generally consists of three essential elements: a socially coherent political community; a mechanism for making authoritative political decisions, that is, a government made up of a corps of officials who act as instruments or in the name of the state; and finally, a body of rules or guidelines, written or unwritten, that set forth the scope of the public authority of the state and the methods by which it is to be exercised by the government.

When a political society, at some stage in its development, settles permanently in specific land areas and subsequently identifies itself with those territories, the conception of the state undergoes an important transformation. The state now becomes characterized as a territorially based political society, where geographic configuration and proximity to other territorial entities become significant factors that affect, and in many cases impose practical limits on, the unifying bonds of kinship and tribal affiliations.

The acquisition of land by the political community will also have the effect of expanding the responsibilities of the state, and may entail a radical revision of its organization and structure. An example of this may be seen in the biblical narrative where the political community of Israel is depicted as functioning through a loose tribal confederation while wandering in the Sinai Desert following its departure from Egypt, but soon adopts a more centralized structure after settling permanently in Canaan. Where arable land or other natural endowments are in short supply, the organization of the state may have to be suitably adjusted to provide a greater ability to protect the territory claimed by the community from the competing claims of other political communities. The growth in the extent of property that is under an individual's control within a society also tends to increase the need and demand for the protection of such holdings by the state. This may involve the need for regulation of the interactions between members of the society, as well as with strangers. As the society develops, particularly as its material wealth grows, its internal structure and relationships may become even more extensive and complex. The regulation of the affairs of such an evolving society will require an ever more elaborately organized administrative structure for the state and its governing institutions. As a rule, the power and scope of the state's jurisdiction tend to expand in direct relation to the growth of the society in its various dimensions.

Parallel to an increasingly elaborate state structure comes an expansion in the definition of the powers of the public authority and the manner in which these are exercised in the name of the state. These definitions of state authority, and the manner in which such authority is manifested in governmental practices, eventually crystallize into fixed customary rules of conduct that represent the public law of a given political society at a particular stage of its development. Notwithstanding the presumed similarity of governmental structures in the earliest stages of state formation, in the course of their actual development states tend to assume widely divergent forms because of their unique historical experiences, geographic configuration, ethnic composition, economic foundations, and other relevant factors.

In modern times there has been an evident tendency for the state to assume an increasingly absolutist role in the life of society, irrespective of its form of government. This development was pointed out by Walter Lippmann in 1929, and his remarks have not lost any of their timeliness.

When I speak of the absolute state, I do not refer to the constitutional arrangement of powers within the state. It is of no importance in this connection whether the absolute power of the state is exercised by a king, a landed aristocracy, bankers and manufacturers, professional politicians, soldiers, or a random majority of voters. It does not matter whether the right to govern is hereditary or obtained with the consent of the governed. A state is absolute in the sense which I have in mind when it claims the right to a monopoly of all force within the community to make war, to make peace, to conscript life, to tax, to establish and disestablish property, to define crime, to punish disobedience, to control education, to supervise the family, to regulate personal habits, and to censor opinions. The modern state claims all these powers, and in the matter of theory there is no real difference in the size of the claim between communists, fascists, and democrats. There are lingering traces in the American constitutional system of the older theory that there are inalienable rights which government may not absorb. But these rights are really not inalienable because they can be taken away by constitutional amendment. There is no theoretical limit upon the power of ultimate majorities which create civil government. There are only practical limits. They are restrained by inertia, and by prudence, even by good will. But ultimately and theoretically they claim absolute authority as against all foreign states, as against all churches, associations, and persons within their jurisdiction.[23]

Such is the modern state as we have come to know it. Our concern in the chapters that follow is to examine the several theories of the genesis of the state and political authority that have been used to justify the powers of the state, and the obligations of obedience to it on the part of its citizens.

2

The Origin of the State

In one form or another, the state has been a pervasive feature of human society throughout all recorded history. In addition, a common characteristic of most politically organized societies has been their routine division into permanent or temporary classes of rulers and subjects. This, plus the universal individual experience of subjugation to the authority of others, makes it tempting to assert that these social phenomena are grounded in the natural order of things. However, the mere fact of their pervasiveness should not in itself be considered as sufficient justification for ungrudging acceptance of this state of affairs as the way things are supposed to be. This is particularly so within the context of Western civilization where the individual is widely presumed to be endowed with intrinsic autonomy of will and the right of personal self-determination, a presumption that does not quite square with the idea that it is natural for him to find himself in a position of subjugation to an external human authority, individual or collective. Accordingly, the question with which the political theorist must grapple is how it came about that the political authority of the state exists and is so universally accepted as natural to human society. Is the state nothing more than an improper usurpation of the individual's natural autonomy, or does it have its origin in some source that justifies its demand for the subservience of those over whom it chooses to assert its authority?

The question of the true origins of the state, that is, the precise means by which actual political societies first came into being and adopted the form of the state, is an issue of great historical and especially anthropological interest. Anthropologists and sociologists seek to understand the origins of the modern state by examining still extant primitive societies and applying, as in the method of Robert H. Lowie, "to primitive and civilized societies alike the principle of continuity and psychic unity and . . . attempt to bridge the gap between them by intermediate steps."[1] One of the more favorably received examples of this approach is the hypothesis put forth by Karl Wittfogel, who suggests that the state, as the institutionalization of patterns of organizational and social control, comes into being on a voluntaristic basis when certain groups of agriculturalists find it expedient for their purposes. This occurs, in his theory, "when an experimenting community of farmers or protofarmers" finds large sources of water in an area that, although presently arid, promises to become fertile if the water resources can be harnessed for agriculture. Under such circumstances, "a number of farmers eager to conquer arid lowlands and plains are forced to invoke the organizational devices which—on the basis of premachine technology—offer the one chance of success: they must work in cooperation with their fellows and subordinate themselves to a directing authority."[2]

Unfortunately, while anthropological and sociological studies and theses may suggest possible processes and patterns of political evolution, they do not appear able to demonstrate conclusively that such have ever actually resulted in the formation of states. Moreover, these approaches have generally proven to be of little interest to most political thinkers, unless they can be adduced to bolster a particular, normative view of the state. As a rule, political theorists who have concerned themselves with the question of the genesis of the state are generally far more interested in determining the way in which the state may reasonably be supposed to have come about rather than the manner in which it actually arose. This is because their primary concern, for the most part, is to discover a rationally acceptable basis upon which to justify or to challenge the nature and extent of the authority of an actually existing state or type of state, and the manner in which that authority is exercised by the institutions and instruments of the state. The questions of the origins and intrinsic character of the state have therefore been considered as issues of great theoretical significance, since they can affect the perceived legitimacy of existing states and their governments, and have been considered in the writings of some of the most important thinkers in the history of political thought.

In ancient China, the prevailing Confucian view was that the state arose as a necessary response to the inherent evil manifested by man in a prepolitical state of nature. This position is argued most clearly by Hsun Tzu, who wrote: "The nature of man is evil. His virtue is only an acquired goodness. Everyone is bent on profit. From following his lust for gain arise strifes and contentions, and the harmony of life is lost." In this view, man is guilty of the relentless and unrestrained pursuit of self-gratification, and in so doing upsets the natural harmony of nature. The undesirable consequences of this include the rapid decline of personal loyalty and fidelity to others and a significant increase in the general level of dissolute conduct. "A total loss of truth and decency ensues, and a cultured life is lost in a carnal spirit. This concupiscence gives birth to strife and discord. Man fails in his duty and there is a constant tendency to revert to savagery. For this reason has it been necessary to have teachers to guide and law to correct him. By their help the spirit of mutual courtesy is fostered, refinement of life cultivated, and an ordered state of society established."[3] The state thus emerges as a moral imperative.

Viewed from this perspective, since man's intrinsic nature does not change over the course of time, the need for the state does not diminish. It therefore remains in existence as a necessary and self-sustaining institution for the ethical purpose of raising and maintaining man at a moral level above that of the savage. However, while there is broad agreement among the classic Chinese teachers on this fundamental idea of why the state came into existence, there is little consensus as to how it came into being, that is, whether the state emerged naturally, through force, or whether it was instituted by Heaven.

During antiquity in the Hellenic world, the state was generally viewed as being a divine creation.[4] Among the early Greeks, who conceived of their gods as intertwined in human affairs, the institutions of government were quite naturally considered as being at least indirectly of divine origin, as were all phenomena. Although men were obviously involved in the formation of the state, it was not considered by the Greek thinkers as being primarily the handiwork of man, but as something that was a necessary consequence of the very nature of man, and a concern of the gods. We see intimations of this in the classic Greek literature. Thus, in the *Iliad* of Homer we find the idea of "right" actions (Themis) personified as a goddess, the embodiment of divine authority, and it is Zeus who grants to kings the authority to rule. In his *Theogony*, Hesiod relates the myth that Zeus wed Themis, who gave birth to Eunomia (Good Order), Diké (Justice), and Eirené (Peace), who represent the basic principles undergirding all human societies.[5] The Greek concern with the search for Eunomia, or the good order of their society, and their conception of the nature of the state led them to consider the state more as an end in itself than as a means for furthering human purposes. As a consequence, the state took on a significance that dwarfed that of its citizens who, for the most part, submitted docilely to its virtually unlimited authority.

At the end of the sixth century B.C., Heraclitus taught that "all human laws are nourished by the one divine law, which prevails as far as it wishes, suffices for all things, and yet is something more than they." Therefore, he concludes, "the people should fight for their law as for their city wall."[6] In the following century, Protagoras propounded a theory of social origins that described three stages of development.

In the first phase, a sort of state of nature, men lived dispersed without benefit of civic association. The consequence of this was that "they were destroyed by the wild beasts, for they were utterly weak in comparison of them, and their art was only sufficient to provide them with the means of life ... but not yet any art of government, of which the art of war is a part. After a while the desire of self-preservation gathered them into cities." They were thus driven to establish civic communities as a matter of necessity, thereby entering the second stage. At this point, however, the fact that they had organized themselves proved of little avail because they still did not possess the art of government. As a result they soon began to encroach upon one another, recreating the chaos and destruction they had experienced earlier. Then, opening the third phase, Zeus became concerned that mankind would destroy itself and decided "to send Hermes to them, bearing reverence and justice to be the ordering principles of cities and the bonds of friendship and conciliation."[7] Thus, the state finally came into existence as a divinely sanctioned expression of the common will. However, Protagoras clearly conceived of the state as an ordinance of God and not as an autonomous creation of man.[8]

By contrast, the Romans were far less inclined to attribute divine origins to the state and, consistent with their more legalistic orientation, they began to draw reasonably clear distinctions between the nature and scope of divine and civil authority. For the Romans, law was a creation of the state, and the source of its ultimate authority was considered to rest with the Roman people. They may therefore have been the first to attempt to assign a definitive legal form to the structure of the state, in effect imposing limits on the authority and power of the government.

One of the few Roman writers to deal explicitly with the question of the origins of the state and political authority was Marcus Tullius Cicero. In his view, the source of all human goods and virtues was to be found in nature, including the natural impulse in man toward association with others. "For the human kind is not solitary, nor do its members live lives of isolated roving; but it is so constituted that, even if it possessed the greatest plenty of material comforts, [it would nevertheless be impelled by its nature to live in social groups.]" This accounts for the emergence of the political association which Cicero defined as "the coming together of a considerable number of men who are united by a common agreement about law and rights and by the desire to participate in mutual advantages."[9] When the people's concerns are directed to the establishment of institutions designed to promote their common interest, this fundamental political association, the *res publica*, the "people's affair" or commonwealth, is given the form of the *civitas*, or the state.[10] "Consequently," Cicero continues, "every people, which is a number of men united in the way I have explained, every state, which is an organization of the people, every commonwealth, which, as I have said, is the people's affair, needs to be ruled by some sort of deliberating authority in order that it may endure." Cicero does not specify what form this authority must take, as long as it is consonant with the "peculiar grounds which have brought the particular state into being." Accordingly, the deliberating authority could "be delegated either to a single man, or to certain selected persons, or it must be retained by all members of the group."[11]

While Cicero does not consider monarchy, aristocracy, or democracy to be ideal forms of government, they are acceptable to him "if the bond holds which originally united its members in the social order of the commonwealth."[12] In his view, the bond that holds the political society together is law. Given the natural diversity among men in character and ability, it is law alone that can be shared equally by all citizens, giving each a mutual stake in the perseverance of the state. What then, he asks, is a state, "if it is not an association of citizens united by law?"[13] It is quite evident that in Cicero's view, where the rule of law does not prevail there can be no state.

Cicero's views, however, did not reflect the consensus of Roman opinion on the genesis of the state. There were also significantly different schools of thought on this question. The Roman historian Tacitus rejected Cicero's thesis concerning man's intrinsically political nature. He suggested instead that men originally lived in a condition of innocence, without any apparent need for political association. "Mankind in the earliest age lived for a time without a single vicious impulse, without shame or guilt, and, consequently, without punishment and restraints. Rewards were not needed when everything right was pursued on its own merits; and as men desired nothing against morality, they were debarred from nothing by fear." This idyllic existence in a state of nature came to an end when, for reasons that Tacitus does not explain, men "began to throw off equality and ambition and violence usurped the place of self-control and modesty, despotisms grew up and became perpetual among many nations. Some from the beginning, or when tired of kings, preferred codes of laws."[14] The implication of this argument is that the state was brought into being by man as a deliberate and logically necessary means for the express purpose of assuring both internal and external peace and security.

The differences between Cicero and Tacitus concerning the basis of the state reflect a fundamental dichotomy of approach to the issue that is characteristic of political thought throughout the ages. Indeed, the wide range of opinions on the question of the genesis of the state and political authority may conveniently be grouped according to how such views respond to the fundamental question of whether the state is a natural or artificial, that is man-made, association. The answer is significant because, as pointed out by William Ernest Hocking, there is a tendency to ascribe greater significance and authority to that which is natural than to what man has created by himself. As a consequence, those who defend the virtually unlimited authority of government have been inclined to claim a natural origin for the state. Hocking suggests that the reason for this is "because to the evolutionary eye, what is made by man may be a mistake, whereas what is made by nature has a putative guarantee of fitness in the world. For the same reason critics of the state, pluralists and anarchists, together with reformers, are prone . . . to dwell on the elements of invention and manufacture in state-building; for whatever is man-made may with advantage be otherwise made, or even unmade."[15]

Although not every theory of the origins of the state fits neatly into the categories of natural or artificial constructs, *these* provide a useful means of making a gross distinction among the variety of approaches to the issue. Most theories of the state do fit comfortably enough within these two broad groupings, although it may prove desirable to establish some sub-divisions that take into consideration the substantial distinctions among the theories that are included within each of the categories. Accordingly, in the chapters that follow, theories of the natural origins of the state are classified as divine, patriarchal, or organic; while those that conceive of the state as an artificial construct are categorized as force or consent theories.

3

The Divine Theory

Upon reflection, it should not at all be surprising that people should turn to the divine theory for an explanation of the origin of the state. Most people, in modern times as in ancient, at some point in their lives feel that they are in the grip of forces over which they can exercise no effective influence. This has been given expression in the popular saying that the only certainties in life are death and taxes. The obvious implications of this are that just as one cannot control the ultimate course of nature, so too is the natural course of the state beyond the reach of the individual. Perhaps precisely because man has felt helpless in the face of the overwhelming power of the state, he has sought to explain it as something that is by its very nature beyond his control, something that has its origin in the supernatural, the divine.

In the Indian classic *The Mahabharata*, the origin of kingship or political authority is set forth by Bhisma in a manner that has distinctive echoes in Catholic political thought some two millennia later. He begins his account by describing the prepolitical state of nature as one of unrelenting chaos and evil. According to Bhisma, in primeval days the people behaved toward one another as though they were fish, the stronger devouring the weaker. As a consequence of this anarchy, no man's life was secure. In an attempt to deal with this problem, the people gathered together, constituting themselves as a political association, and established a common regime to assure their mutual and personal security. They concluded a social compact which effectively stipulated that whosoever might be found guilty of the abuse of another, assault, adultery, or robbery would be cast out of the community.

However, it was not long before they discovered that the compact they had agreed to was not self-enforcing, and since they had no means by which to ensure compliance with the agreement, they continued to suffer from anarchy and the concomitant social chaos. Recognizing the weakness of their attempt to resolve their problems in this manner, they collectively appealed for help to the Grand-sire Brahma. Pleading that they were faced by destruction, they prayed for Brahma to send them a lord and master who would protect them, one whom they would collectively honor. He subsequently designated the patriarch Manu for the task.

Manu, however, declined the appointment. He told the people that he was unable to accept the responsibility because of a general distaste for the task of government, as well as the great difficulties he expected to encounter in ruling over people who were corrupt by their very nature. To encourage Manu to change his mind and accept the responsibility of ruling them, the people contracted an agreement with him that assured him of their complete support. As tangible evidence of the latter, they agreed to compensate him with the payment of one fifth of their livestock and cash, one tenth of the crops that were held in common, and to provide him with a bodyguard. Moreover, while each individual would be held personally liable for his transgressions, Manu would earn a one fourth share of all the merit derived from the positive acts performed by the people as a consequence of the protection he gave them. This lopsided proposal, whereby the king was absolved of any responsibility for the transgressions of his subjects while being guaranteed a rather large share of their merits, was too favorable for

Manu to refuse. After concluding the agreement, he sallied forth with his troops, striking terror into the hearts of all evil-doers, subduing the wicked and directing the people to pursue their respective occupations and to fulfill their obligations.

This ancient narrative may be seen as setting forth "the doctrine of the king's Divine creation reinforced by the theory of a Governmental Compact of a distinctly unilateral character between the people and the King-designate."[1] It will be noted that this theory of the origin of the state is quite similar in a number of respects to that suggested by Protagoras (See Chapter 2), particularly with regard to his description of the three phases of social development into the state.

The divine theory is also found in the *Manusmriti*, but in a more restrictive formulation. Manu accepts the idea of the divine creation of the king as a necessary corrective to the consequences of anarchy in the world, which is in itself presumably a result of the varying natures of men with respect to their virtues and faults. Thus Manu states: "When these creatures, being without a king, through fear dispersed in all directions, the Lord created a king for the protection of the world." This king, who was compounded from the eternal particles of the eight deities, "surpasses all created beings in lustre; and like the sun, he burns eyes and hearts; nor can anybody on earth even gaze on him."[2]

Notwithstanding this apotheosis of the state, and its implicit absolutism, Manu insists that the king who oppresses his subjects negates the very purpose for which his kingship was instituted in the first place. Although the people have no option other than to obey, the king who rules tyrannically will nonetheless come to an ignominious end. "That king who through folly rashly oppresses his kingdom [will], together with his relatives, ere long be deprived of his life and of his kingdom. As the lives of living creatures are destroyed by tormenting their bodies, even so the lives of kings are destroyed by their oppressing their kingdoms." This has been interpreted by some as suggesting that the people retain some residual rights against the king and may oppose him. However, this is a matter of contention among scholars, some of whom deny the existence of a concept of political or civil rights in traditional Hindu political thought.[3]

A similar theory of the divine origin of the state is expounded in another Hindu classic, the *Sukranitisara*. Although Sukra too describes the king as having been created from the eternal particles of the eight deities, he differs from Manu primarily in that he does not consider the king to have become a god; he is only similar to the gods. He also indicates that a ruler who fails to meet his responsibilities should be repudiated or even expelled by the people, and that another prince of the same dynasty should be installed by the royal priest to protect the people.[4] Once again, the question of whether Sukra should be understood as implying that the people retain an inherent right of revolution is a matter of substantial scholarly disagreement.

In the Graeco-Roman world, for as long as the question of the origin of the state was only a matter of intellectual curiosity, speculation unrelated to any of the practical political issues of the day, it was treated rather casually. This has been the general pattern throughout the history of political philosophy, vigorously argued theories tending to evolve only in response to the demands of contemporary events and conditions. The power of the state was a given, and the origins and sources of that power mattered little as a practical matter. This situation changed significantly, however, with the acquisition of temporal power by the church. The subsequent power struggle between the pope and the secular emperor made the issue of the divine or non-divine origin of political authority and power a matter of considerable importance, and consequently a subject of intense interest.

During its early history, the church was evidently and avowedly an institution that claimed exclusive dominion only over the spiritual interests of mankind, attaching little importance to the state. In the New Testament teaching, the state is not regarded as an institution of such ultimate significance to man that it is somehow to be equated with the kingdom of God on earth. On the contrary, the state is considered as a structure that is clearly temporary in nature.

It belongs to the contemporary age of man, and it is one of
those institutions that will most assuredly lose its reason for
existence with the arrival of the kingdom of God. This being
the case, Jesus's disciples have the right as well as the duty
to render judgment on the state on the basis of their knowledge of the coming kingdom and the will of God. However,
as long as the present age persists, the continued existence
of the profane state, even the heathen and anti-Christian
Roman state, is considered to be a reflection of the divine
will. It is therefore deemed inappropriate for the disciple of
Jesus to take any initiative in attempting to abolish the essentially secular institution of the state. Instead, he is obligated to render to the state whatever support it needs for
its subsistence. But, once the state presumes to demand more
than it can reasonably justify as necessary for its existence,
it trespasses beyond the limits of its proper authority and
usurps that which is God's. Under such circumstances, the
disciple of Jesus is relieved of any divinely ordained obligation to satisfy such an unjust and excessive demand. Indeed, he is duty-bound to proclaim that the state has
transgressed its proper limits and has demanded what belongs to God. However, while he may resist providing to
the state that which it unjustly demands of him, he will
nonetheless remain obligated to continue to pay the usual
taxes to it. In other words, the state's excesses do not invalidate its legitimate requirements; the Christian may not
use the occasion of refusing the state's unjust demands to
also refuse those that are proper. Furthermore, the disciple
of Jesus will not take it upon himself to challenge the state
by force of arms in the name of the Gospel.[5] In this regard,
Paul states explicitly:

Let every person be subject to the governing authorities. For there
is no authority except from God, and those that exist have been
instituted by God. Therefore he who resists the authorities resists
what God has appointed, and those who resist will incur judgment.
For rulers are not a terror to good conduct, but to bad. Would
you have no fear of him who is in authority? Then do what is
good, and you will receive his approval, for he is God's servant

for your good. But if you do wrong, be afraid, for he does not bear the sword in vain; he is the servant of God to execute his wrath on the wrongdoer. Therefore one must be subject, not only to avoid God's wrath but also for the sake of conscience. For the same reason you also pay taxes, for the authorities are ministers of God, attending to this very thing. Pay all of them their dues, taxes to whom taxes are due, revenue to whom revenue is due, honor to whom honor is due.[6]

Similarly, the patristic writings clearly taught obedience to the state in all things not contrary to the law of God. The Church Fathers freely admitted the supremacy of the civil power in all temporal matters. During the early period of the development of the church, the fundamental principle upon which relations between the church and the state were to be conducted was, "Render therefore to Caesar the things that are Caesar's, and to God the things that are God's."[7] This was understood by Ambrose to mean: "If the Emperor demand tribute, we should not refuse. . . . If the Emperor desire our fields, he has the power to take them, no one of us can resist. . . . We will pay to Caesar that which is Caesar's."[8]

Yet, notwithstanding its presumably divine origin, the secular power was not considered as constituting a sacred institution. Thus, in the second century, Irenaeus described the secular powers as those who "have been appointed by God for the utility of the Gentiles."[9] In other words, there is no doubt that the secular powers are in fact ministers of God, but Irenaeus considers them to be essentially "Gentile" powers. Their divinely originated powers were not intended for the disciples of Jesus, but only for the Gentiles, that is, the non-Christians. As Gerard Caspary observes:

No doubt, good Christians would be murdered in their beds, or at least deprived of all the necessities of life, if such powers had not been appointed to lord it over the kingdoms of the Gentiles. . . . From that perspective, both powers, the Christian power of the bishops within the Church and the Gentile power, the power of kings without, are equally necessary; both have been established by God, the one through Christ, the other through the original act of creation of the world. Yet the royal power is not seen as either in the sacramental penumbra of the Church or as a demonic entity in the darkness without; it is seen instead as an essentially pre-Christian, 'secular,' power appointed primarily for the utility of those who do not yet belong—or at least do not yet fully belong—to the People of God.[10]

For Origen, Paul's teaching served as authority for making a clear, though in no sense necessarily antagonistic, distinction between church and state. There are hints in his teachings that he considered the ministerial role assigned to the state in early Christianity as somewhat paradoxical given the essential antithesis between God and the world. However, this dimension of the church-state relationship, while remaining in the background, is not given any prominence by Origen. Instead, church and state are treated as essentially parallel structures, both equally part of a dual hierarchy that culminates in God. While the distinctions between the two institutions are clearly drawn, there is as yet no explicit emphasis given to the contrasts between their methods or functions, nor are they seen as potential antagonists.[11]

This approach is more fully developed in the works of Augustine, who drew the distinctions between the state and the church even more sharply. For him, by contrast with Irenaeus, the state and its coercive powers are divinely ordained to serve as remedies for the sinful condition of fallen man, including the adherents of the church. Indeed, in Augustine's view, it is the inherent sinfulness of man that necessitates the establishment of the state to impose peace and order in the temporal world. Even though its ability to achieve these purposes may be limited, the state is nonetheless to be seen as a divine gift to man. Accordingly, the authority of the ruler is established by divine mandate and the extent of his power may not be curtailed by those over whom he has been designated to exercise dominion. Thus, "when Christians render obedience to rulers they are really obeying God rather than men, since it is God who establishes rulers and who orders that they be obeyed."[12]

In the seventh century, the divine theory of the state received new impetus with the rise of Islam, which conceived the true source of political authority to be in "the will of God as manifested in the *shari'ah* [Islamic law]."[13] This is reflected in the following teaching of the Qur'an: "Say: O Allah! Owner of Sovereignty! Thou givest sovereignty unto whom Thou wilt, and Thou withdrawest sovereignty from whom Thou wilt. Thou exaltest whom Thou wilt and Thou abasest whom Thou wilt. In Thy hand is the good. Lo! Thou art able to do all things."[14] In the traditional teachings of Islam the Prophet is reported to have amplified this by stating: "He who obeys me, obeys God; and he who disobeys me, disobeys God. And he who obeys the *amir* (i.e., the head of the state), obeys me; and he who disobeys the *amir*, disobeys me."[15]

The divine origin of the state, unadorned by any notion of popular involvement in the process, was argued unequivocally in the eleventh century by the vizir of Seljuqid Persia. Nizam al-Mulk wrote: "In every age and time God (be He exalted) chooses one member of the human race and, having adorned and endowed him with kingly virtues, entrusts him with the interests of the world and the well-being of His servants; He charges that person to close the doors of corruption, confusion and discord, and He imparts to him such dignity and majesty in the eyes and hearts of men, that under his just rule they may live their lives in constant security and ever wish for his reign to continue."[16] This same idea is echoed some years later in the writing of John of Salisbury, who states: "According to the usual definition, the prince is the public power, and a kind of likeness on earth of the divine majesty. Beyond doubt a large share of the divine power is shown to be in princes by the fact that at their nod men bow their necks and for the most part offer up their heads to the axe to be struck off . . . And this I do not think could be, except as a result of the will of God. For all power is from the Lord God."[17]

In consideration of his influence on much of subsequent Catholic political thought, it is of particular interest to note that Thomas Aquinas made a significant departure from patristic doctrine and the consensus of scholastic opinion with regard to the question of the origin of the state. By sharp contrast with his predecessors, who attributed the genesis of political authority to the fallen state of mankind, Aquinas, taking a position akin to that of Cicero, insisted that "it is natural for man, more than for any other animal, to be a social and political animal, to live in a group. . . . If, then, it is natural for man to live in the society of many, it is necessary that there exist among men some means by which the group may be governed. For where there are many men together and each one is looking after his own interest, the multitude would be broken up and scattered unless there were also an agency to take care of what appertains to the common-weal."[18]

By asserting that the ultimate emergence of the state was inherent in man's essential nature and not solely due to his fallen state as a consequence of Original Sin, Aquinas lay the groundwork for the view that the role of the state went beyond that of merely serving as the policeman for a corrupt and violent society; it was also a positive force for directing men toward the good life. This synthesis of traditional church teaching and the classic Greek view of the ethical role of the state had a profound impact on later European political thought.[19]

It did not take very long before the inevitable conflict between the church and the state began to take clear shape. The seeds of that confrontation lay in the very foundations of the church. By proclaiming the kingdom of God, the church effectively declared that man had liberty of conscience. This was necessary in order to give the individual an autonomy with regard to spiritual matters that was beyond and superior to the claims of the state. However, as the papacy increased its power and influence, the church began to claim authority over matters that went beyond the spiritual and encroached on the secular. Thus, it soon asserted the right of intervention to preserve the peace and to adjudicate disputes between the temporal Christian rulers. It undertook to safeguard and enforce public and private morality, and to give effect to its decisions through the use of the powerful instruments of anathema and excommunication, and, when necessary, the sword.

The temporal power of the church increased incrementally until it took on the role of a civic institution itself, becoming a veritable state, albeit without a clearly defined territory. Like other states, it promulgated civil laws and used military power to coerce obedience. Before long, it began to compete with the temporal rulers for the right of supreme control over Christian Europe. The great minds of medieval Europe became engrossed and engaged in the dramatic and far reaching struggle for power. Dante, William of Occam, and Marsilius of Padua put their pens to work in defense of the claims of the temporal powers, while Hincmar, Hildebrand, Thomas Aquinas, and Giles of Rome took up their pens in support of the broad political pretensions of the papacy. Throughout the long acrimonious struggle, the papal and temporal powers continued to share a common perspective on at least one point: namely, that the institutions and authorities of both church and state derived from the divine order of the universe. The protracted conflict, therefore, was not over the question of the ultimate nature and source of political authority; it was concerned only with the issue of how and to whom it was delegated by the supreme author.

The Protestant Reformation, rather than helping to dispel the confusion that had resulted from the various approaches to dealing with the vexing problem of where the locus of political authority lay, contributed to further exacerbating it. Its leaders, Luther, Melanchthon, Zwingli, and Calvin, reasserted the divine origin of political authority and insisted upon the absolute necessity of obedience to the state. In his tract on *Secular Authority*, and again in his *Address to the German Nobility*, Luther proclaimed the doctrine that "the state is a necessity to man, that it has existed from the beginnings of the race, and that it—i.e., not any one particular state, nor any one particular government or form of government, but the *state*—is as necessary a part of the divine plan or economy for the benefit of the external life of man in society as the institution of the church."[20] By insisting that the state was a necessary element of the divine plan for the benefit and salvation of man's immortal soul, Luther categorically denied that the state was in any way dependent on the church. It had its own independent divine origin. Calvin, echoing the argument of Thomas Aquinas but drawing rather different conclusions from it, affirmed that "the authority possessed by kings and other governors over all things upon earth is not a consequence of the perverseness of men but of the providence and holy ordinance of God, who has been pleased to regulate human affairs in this manner; for as much as he is present, and also presides among them, in making laws and in executing equitable judgments."[21] To counter this onslaught, their Catholic opponents, particularly the Dominicans and Jesuits, were now forced to reverse their traditional positions that postulated a divine source of the state. They now devoted their energies to demonstrating the purely mundane character of the state. This became necessary in order to restrict the claims of spiritual origin and divine authority exclusively to the church. In this way, they could argue that the temporal political authority must be seen as subordinate to that of the divinely sanctioned church.

As Catholic political thought evolved, it tended to distinguish two rather different approaches to the question of the origin of political authority—the designation theory and the translation theory. The designation theory asserts that political authority is transferred to its holder by God, but not by direct divine intervention in human affairs. Instead, it postulates that God works through normal human social processes, which in this instance may include the spontaneous agreement of the people, or an expression of the popular will, through an electoral process. But, as Heinrich Rommen points out, "these human acts are not the cause of the transfer of authority; they are only the condition, the naturally necessary condition, of the transfer that proceeds immediately from God to the holder of authority. Therefore, when the fathers of families institute the state, authority does not in any way, even for a moment, rest with the people as a unity being organized into a body politic."[22] The implications of the designation theory are that a group of people, upon being transformed into a body politic, has a duty to identify a person with naturally superior gifts of leadership as the one most suitable to wield sovereign political authority. In this way, without any direct divine intervention, the transfer of divine authority is carried out in a providential manner by the citizens of the new body politic. The supporters of this theory emphatically do not conceive of it as a form of contract theory (to be discussed later). The expression of the popular will is strictly limited to the designation of the person or persons who will exercise sovereign authority; it does not involve any agreement with respect to the nature of the rule to which they will be subjected. Moreover, in consonance with the idea that this transfer process accords with the divinely ordained natural order of things, the people are not considered as having the option of not choosing a sovereign.

By contrast with the preceding, the translation theory argues that, at the moment of constitution of the body politic, political authority is transferred by God directly to the body politic itself. This is because, in principle, all men are born free and equal and no one individual merits being invested with such authority in preference to another. The political authority, which comes into being simultaneously with the formation of the political society, remains with the community itself for as long as it is not transferred, and the members of the body politic are under no compulsion by natural law to transfer this authority away from their collective selves. Therefore, according to the translation theory, "in order that a certain individual may become the holder of sovereign authority, the originally immediate (non-representative) democracy must by a free act of the people be transformed into another constitutional form. Consequently, no ruler holds his authority by natural law, but by human law."[23] The translation theory is thus clearly a unique compound of divine theory and social contract theory.

The translation theory, which became quite popular in modern Catholic political thought, was perhaps best articulated in the sixteenth century by Francisco Suarez. He argued, in essence, that since a community obviously needs some sort of regime to prevent social chaos, God has given it the power to govern itself.

Nature is never lacking in essentials; therefore, just as a perfect community is in harmony with reason and natural law, so, too, is the power to govern it, without which there would be in such a community the greatest possible confusion. For each individual member looks after his own interests, which are often opposed to the common good; also there are many things necessary for the common good but not relevant to individual needs . . . Hence, in a perfect society, there must be some public power whose official duty is to consider and provide for the common good.[24]

There is, however, a fundamental problem since, as Suarez points out, "all men are by nature born free and no one has political authority over anyone else by the very essence of their nature."[25] That is, men are intrinsically equal and, in accordance with natural law, no one possesses the inherent right to wield political authority over his fellow man, nor is any one individual intrinsically more entitled than another to be the person entrusted with such authority. This position was already clearly set forth in the writing of Nicholas of Cusa, who argued that "since all are by nature free, then every rulership whether it is by written law or by living law through a prince, which restrains the subjects from evil and directs their freedom to good through fear of punishment can only come from the agreement and consent of the subjects. For if, by nature, men are equally powerful and equally free, a true and properly ordered authority of one common ruler who is equal in power can only be naturally constituted by the election and consent of the others."[26]

Suarez then argues that "if, therefore, this power does not reside in a specific individual, it must necessarily reside in the whole community." Just as man, by the fact and circumstance of his creation, is naturally free and has power over himself, so too does the political community have power over itself once it is brought into existence. "Men as a whole ought then rather to be considered from the angle of that special will, or common consent, through which they come together into a body politic in the bond of society for mutual aid towards a single political end." Having thus constituted a political society, men are confronted by an intractable dilemma. The viability of the community requires that it have a central authority, sufficiently powerful to overcome any challenges to it from the recalcitrant. However, the establishment of such a central locus of power also requires each member of the society to subordinate himself to it, surrendering his autonomy. Man must choose between the alternatives of retaining his freedom with social chaos or subjugating himself to the body politic in exchange for the security it offers. He cannot have both simultaneously. "It is impossible to imagine a unified political body without either political government or a disposition towards it, because their very unity comes, to a considerable extent, from subjection to the same rule and a common superior power; and again, without it, the body could not be directed towards one end and the common good. It is repugnant to reason to think of a human community in one body politic which has no common power that individual members of the community must obey."[27]

In discussing the matter of political authority, Suarez draws an analogy between parents and the political society. He argues that just as the will and intervention of the parents are necessary only for procreation of the child but are not intrinsically involved in the grant of natural freedom to their offspring, so too are the will and consent of the community necessary for the formation of the body politic but not in order to endow the political society with its fundamental authority. That authority is a necessary consequence of the body politic's inherent nature, which is determined by God. In this sense, political authority has a divine origin.[28]

Suarez insists that original political authority rests with the body politic in the form of direct self-government, which is essentially democratic in nature.[29] Except in the case where the original democracy is overthrown through conquest by an alien force, any legitimate change in the status of the body politic can properly take place only with the consent of the citizens; they alone can surrender their democracy and transfer its political authority to a particular person or group of persons. Consequently, where one finds political authority being held by a person or persons other than the citizenry as a whole, it is assumed that there must have been a voluntary transfer of such authority by the people as a whole, either formally or informally. In those instances where the community elects to surrender it, such a decision is presumed to have been made as a matter of expediency rather than from any natural necessity, as is maintained by the designation theory.[30]

Moreover, Suarez asserts, even though the appointment of a ruler and the transfer of the community's authority to him is a matter of human law, "once power has been transferred to the king, he is at once the vicar of God and by natural law must be obeyed . . . he is by that very power made superior even to the kingdom which granted it; for in giving it the kingdom subjected itself and deprived itself of its former liberty." However, this grant of power is not entirely unconditional. Should the king turn to tyranny, that would constitute grounds for a legitimate revolt against his power. Thus, "when this power has been transferred to a particular person, even if it passes several times by succession or various elections to different people, the community must still be understood to retain immediate possession of it, because by force of its first action the community transferred it to the rest." Except with respect to the matter of tyranny, which invalidates the transfer, "this transference of power from the community to the prince is not a delegation but almost an abrogation, a total grant of all that power which was formerly in the community.[31]

The fundamental character of the church-state controversy underwent a major transformation as a result of the Reformation. It soon changed from one that was primarily a struggle for supremacy between ecclesiastical and temporal power to a class conflict between the rulers and the ruled. The critical issue for political thinkers was no longer that of the origin of political authority. That had been resolved to some extent by the growing acceptance of the translation theory, namely, that all currently existing political authority and power originated in a freely awarded contractual gift of the community. Instead, the focus of attention turned to the question of the scope and character of such political authority as it was exercised by actual rulers. The essential points of concern were the terms and implications of the postulated contract between the ruled and their rulers. The central issue was whether in transferring its authority the community had totally and irrevocably alienated its autonomy, or whether it had merely made a revocable delegation of supreme political power to the ruler, as suggested by Suarez. The implications of the latter position were revolutionary, and threatened to undermine the legitimacy of existing regimes.

This new controversy forced radical changes in the relations between church and state. The same temporal rulers who, when struggling with the papacy for supremacy, were quite willing to dispense entirely with the sanction or support of the church, now sought to enlist the spiritual power and moral authority of the church to help preserve their regimes. They needed the church to bolster their legitimacy by condemning tyrannicide and the overthrow of unpopular rulers as unacceptable before God. At the same time, many of the clergy in France and other countries, whose rulers remained loyal to the papacy, now refused to accept the full consequences of the very theories of contract and natural law that they had been willing enough to support earlier, during the church's struggles against the temporal rulers, when so doing served their purposes. Although the divine theory remained a staple of Catholic political thought, it soon fell into neglect in Protestant circles in favor of other approaches, such as contract theory and patriarchalism.

In essence, the divine theory of the genesis of the state justifies political authority in general as deriving from God, and lends legitimacy to the exercise of political power by particular individuals, who are presented as agents of the divine will, either by direct or indirect delegation of divinely sanctioned authority. However, the theory is seriously flawed and therefore difficult to sustain. By stipulating that *all* power derives from God, the theory allows anyone who aspires to political power to assert that his inclinations are also of divine origin and of equal standing with that of the established political authorities, entitling him to the same legitimacy irrespective of prevailing law or custom in a particular political society. Furthermore, as argued by Ibn Khaldun, with respect to the Judaeo-Christian-Muslim conception of deity, the theory is simply incapable of demonstration, because he considers it self-evident that "human society can exist without such a Divine Law, merely in virtue of the authority imposed by one man or of the social solidarity which compels the others to follow and obey him." He argues that the number of people who are actually monotheists, believing in a single all-powerful deity are few "in comparison with the pagans, who do not have a book and who constitute a majority of the inhabitants of the world. And yet these pagans have not only lived but have founded states and left monuments. . . . Their condition is therefore not one of anarchy, i.e., of men left to themselves without restraint, for such a condition cannot possibly exist."[32]

While the divine theory of the state has generally fallen into disregard in the West, it has recently gained new vitality in the Muslim world, with the growth of Islamic fundamentalism as a political force. Thus, in 1969–1970, the late Ayatollah Ruhollah Khomeini, commenting on the role of law in ordering the good society, stated: "A collection of laws is not enough to reform society. . . . This is why God, may He be praised, created on earth, in addition to the laws, a government and an executive and administrative agency." Accordingly, the Prophet "appointed, on orders from God, a successor to carry out these tasks after him. This appointment of a successor indicates clearly the need for government after the Prophet to continue. Considering that this appointment of a successor was on orders from God, then the continuation of government and of its agencies and organizations is also ordered by God."[33]

4

The Patriarchal Theory

Since ancient times, there has been a tendency among some to speak of the emergence of political society as a natural extension of the common experience of patriarchal authority within the context of the family. To this school of thought, which dates back to remote antiquity, the political society in its authoritative embodiment as the state is conceived as the family writ large. The ancient Chinese *I Ching*, in discussing the formation and development of society, states: "Heaven and earth existing, all material things then got their existence. All material things having existence, afterwards there came male and female. From the existence of male and female there came afterwards husband and wife. From husband and wife there came father and son. From father and son there came sovereign and subjects."[1] This is taken as a clear expression of the view, later articulated by Confucius, that the state, as is the case with all the other institutions and related aspects of civilization, is created through a process of phenomenal imitation.

To Confucius the state is an enlarged family, and the formal relationship of the individual to the state may be derived by analogy from the establishment of the appropriate relations between the several members of the family. What, he asks, is meant by the teaching that "in order rightly to govern the State, it is necessary first to regulate the family?" Confucius's response is: "It is not possible for one to teach others, while he cannot teach his own family. Therefore, the ruler, without going beyond his family, completes the lessons of the State. There is filial piety: therewith the sovereign should be served. There is paternal submission: therewith elders and superiors should be served. There is kindness: therewith the multitude should be treated." In other words, the family represents the model of the proper relationships of authority and subservience that are to be imitated on a societal level. "From the loving example of one family, love extends throughout the State; from its courtesy, courtesy extends throughout the State; while the ambition and perverse recklessness of one man may plunge the entire State into rebellion and disorder."[2] Confucian political theory thus views the state as an extended family, and the individual family as the state in miniature. Governmental codes of public regulations are conceived as extensions of family codes of conduct. Public education, which is highly valued, is seen essentially as an extension of family education. Authority and obedience are considered as necessary to the existence of the political order as they are to maintaining the order of family life. In the Confucian view, the state clearly represents a natural stage in the evolution of social life from the patriarchal foundations of the family.[3] As stated in the *Shu King*: "Heaven and earth is the parent of all creatures; and of all creatures man is the most highly endowed. The sincere, intelligent, and perspicacious among men becomes the great sovereign; and the great sovereign is the parent of the people."[4]

In the Hellenic world, somewhat later, Aristotle independently undertook to demonstrate that the household or family is a natural unit, and that the village and subsequently the political society or polis (city-state) is an outgrowth of the family household, thereby making the polis itself a natural form of association. "First of all," he argued, "there must necessarily be a union or pairing of those who cannot exist without one another. Male and female must unite for the reproduction of the species." This establishes a first naturally necessary human association. "Next," according to the Greek philosopher, "there must necessarily be a union of the naturally ruling element with the element which is naturally ruled, for the preservation of both." The argument he makes here, quite unacceptable to many in our own time but which was the conventional wisdom until rather recently, is that the male is the natural superior to the female and that the rule of the superior over the inferior is itself inherent in the natural order of things. These two fundamental associations bring into being the "household or family." The next more extensive form of association is that of the village, which Aristotle considers essentially as a colony or offshoot of a large, presumably extended, family. "When we come to the final and perfect association, formed from a number of villages, we have already reached the polis . . . Because it is the completion of associations existing by nature, every polis exists by nature, having itself the same quality as the earlier associations from which it grew. . . . From these considerations it is evident that the polis belongs to the class of things that exist by nature, and that man is by nature an animal intended to live in a polis."[5]

It has been suggested by some that it is an overstatement of Aristotle's true position to employ his argument as the basis for a patriarchal theory of the origin of the state, since he drew evident distinctions between the natures of familial and political power.[6] In fact, in the sixteenth century Jean Bodin criticized the Greek philosopher for having "divorced economy or household management from police or disciplinary power, without good reason to my mind."[7] Nonetheless, Aristotle's statements do appear to lend themselves to such appropriation, and it is beyond the scope of this work to undertake a full assessment of the validity of counting the philosopher among the progenitors of the patriarchal theory.

The organic connection between the family and the state was accepted by Cicero, who agreed that the family is "the foundation of civil government, the nursery, as it were, of the state," even though he insisted that a common will and

sense of fellowship were still necessary for a state, notwithstanding its natural origin in the family.[8] This same conception was generally held in Europe from the early Christian
period to the Renaissance, and beyond. At the onset of the
sixteenth century, Desiderius Erasmus rejected the notion
that one could draw any significant distinctions between familial and political power. Instead, he wrote: "The good prince
ought to have the same attitude toward his subjects, as a
good *paterfamilias* toward his household—for what else is a
kingdom but a great family? What is the king if not the father
to a great multitude?"[9] Similarly, Bodin argued that "the
well-ordered family is a true image of the commonwealth,
and domestic comparable with sovereign authority. It follows
that the household is the model of right order in the commonwealth. And just as the whole body enjoys health when
every particular member performs its proper function, so all
will be well with the commonwealth when families are properly regulated."[10] Nonetheless, as will be seen later, even
though he accepts a patriarchalist view of the functions of
the state, Bodin also subscribes to the force theory of the
origin of the state.

Perhaps the outstanding advocate of patriarchalism was
the seventeenth century political writer Sir Robert Filmer,
who insisted that the source of all government and political
authority derived from the divine dispensation of sovereignty
originally granted to Adam. He wrote that God centered
"all Power (of Families, Societies, Kingdoms) in one Supreme and Paternall Head, both for perfection and permanence: So as all other Forms argue not only weakness in,
but tend to the perversion, nay subversion . . . because not
agreeing to the Model, which God first erected in Adam.
For even there he established Regal and Paternall Power,
that differ only in proportion, not similitude; (it being the
same, as a Child is a Man in little)."[11] As observed by Gordon
J. Schochet, "Filmer's patriarchalism is an extreme example
of the preoccupation of seventeenth-century English political
philosophy with origins. This attitude dictated that political
obligation could be found in, and had to be consistent with,
the beginnings of government. As used by Filmer and many

other writers, origins referred to the beginnings of political authority *per se* rather than the establishment of a specific state."[12]

The durability of the patriarchal concept is reflected in its continued advocacy by Henry St. John Bolingbroke in the early eighteenth century. Bolingbroke asserted that "civil governments were formed not by the concurrence of individuals, but by the associations of families."[13] In the second half of the nineteenth century, Henry J. S. Maine argued on the basis of his historical researches that the vestiges of the ascending series of groups from the family to the state could be seen in most of the Greek city-states and in Rome. In the latter, the house and the tribe represented the intermediate steps between the family and the state. "The elementary group is the Family, connected by common subjection to the highest male ascendant. The aggregation of families forms the Gens or House. The aggregation of Houses makes the Tribe. The aggregation of Tribes constitutes the commonwealth." This raises the question as to whether it is reasonable to suggest that the state represents a collection of persons united by common descent from the patriarch of the original family. Maine answers: "Of this we may at least be certain, that all ancient societies regarded themselves as having proceeded from one original stock, and even labored under an incapacity for comprehending any reason except this for their holding together in political union. The history of political ideas begins, in fact, with the assumption that kinship in blood is the sole possible ground of community in political functions."[14] He nonetheless acknowledges that not all societies were actually formed by descent from a common ancestor, but suggests that "all of them which had any permanence and solidity either were so descended or assumed that they were."[15]

The patriarchal theory was still being argued at the turn of the twentieth century by William S. Lilly: "Of civil society the family is the germ. The authority of the father, king over his own children, is, as a mere matter of historical fact, the earliest form of the *jus imperandi*. And the patriarchal state is everywhere the primitive polity. The archaic king, or au-

tocratic chieftain, is, if I may so express it, the artificially
extended father. The regal power is but the paternal power
in a wider sphere. . . . History, then, shows us the family as
the origin of the State."[16]

However, despite the long history of the patriarchal theory, and its vigorous defense by Maine and others, there is
little historical evidence to support the contention that the
state is essentially a natural extension of the family. It is
quite true that there are a number of analogies that may be
drawn between certain aspects of family life and political
life, particularly during the early stages of political development in many societies when families rather than individuals were considered to be the fundamental societal building
blocks. Under those circumstances, family interests surely
served as a primary motive force for political decision and
societal action. Patriarchal authority acted to enforce conformity by family members with the norms and rules of conduct that prevailed in the society. Consequently, it appears
reasonable to conjecture that the patterns and modes of
parental authority within the traditional family structure
were appropriated for the subsequent organization of the
rudimentary state. But, it is one thing to argue that analogies
may be drawn between the patriarchal character of the family
and the monarchical character of early states, and quite another matter to insist that political society is a natural development and extension of this small social unit. Jeremy
Bentham, for one, took strong issue with the latter proposition toward the end of the eighteenth century. It is true,
he argued, that every person, at least during the period of
his childhood, and certainly until he has learned to cope with
the requirements of everyday living, is necessarily in a state
of subjection to his parents or to those who stand in the
position of the parents with respect to him. But, he insists,
the analogy to the state is a decidedly poor one. When people
speak of a *political* society, they have something in mind that
is quite unlike a family. "To constitute what is meant in
general by that phrase, a greater number of members is
required, or, at least, a *duration* capable of a longer contin-
uance. Indeed, for this purpose nothing less, I take it, than

an *indefinite* duration is required. A society, to come within the notion of what is originally meant by a *political* one, must be such as, in its nature, is not incapable of continuing forever in virtue of the principles which gave it birth. This, it is plain, is not the case with such a family society, of which a parent, or a pair of parents are at the head."[17]

Bentham's point, of course, is that children grow up and eventually come out from under the umbrella of parental authority. Consequently, the analogy between the family and political society simply does not hold. Furthermore, and notwithstanding certain superficial similarities, the two institutions are also quite different in other fundamental respects as well. As observed by Westel W. Willoughby, the two institutions are distinguished with regard to the sources of their authority. In the family, where the organizing principle is that of subordination, the location of authority is quite naturally with the father. But in the state, where members are essentially equal, the location of authority is a matter of deliberate choice. He concludes that the purposes of the two institutions are so dissimilar "that one could not have owed its origin to the other. The family never was and never can become a subject of public law. Its interests are necessarily private."[18] Edward Jenks felt impelled to voice the strongest possible criticism of the patriarchal theory. "No fallacy," he wrote, "has more confused the study of social history than the sentimental doctrine that the State is an 'enlarged family'; and no honest person in the least familiar with the history of social development could possibly maintain such a doctrine. The State is the very antithesis of the family, and of all institutions based on principles of kinship."[19]

This latter position is argued forcefully by José Ortega y Gasset, who categorically rejected the notion that the state is "like the horde or tribe or other societies based on consanguinity which Nature takes on itself to form without the collaboration of human effort. On the contrary," he insists, "the State begins when man strives to escape from the natural society of which he has been made a member by blood. And by blood, we might also say any other natural principle: language, for example."[20]

Ortega maintains that there is nothing whatsoever that is natural about the state. It is entirely the conscious and deliberate creation of man. He suggests that in a precivic condition man lives in small groups, the social form of which provides for an "internal" existence in common. However, the isolation of these groups is disrupted by economic circumstances, which create situations where individuals enter into relations with others from different social groups, thus creating an "external" common life as well. Powered by incompatible motivations, a disequilibrium emerges between the "internal" and "external" existences. The established social forms of the group, its laws, customs, and religion, tend to favor the "internal" and make it difficult for the "external," which offers the promise of a more ample existence, to take root. "In this situation, the State-principle is the movement which tends to annihilate the social forms of internal existence, and to substitute for them a social form adequate to the new life, lived externally." Accordingly, Ortega asserts, there is no possibility of the state arising unless sufficient people are capable of abandoning the traditional structures of their "internal" existences for a new form of common life. They must break the bonds of family ties in favor of an extrafamilial association. This is why the state must be understood as a genuine act of human creativity and not as a natural extension of the family. "The State begins by being absolutely a work of imagination. Imagination is the liberating power possessed by man. A people is capable of becoming a State in the degree in which it is able to imagine. Hence it is that with all peoples there has been a limit to their evolution in the direction of a State: precisely the limit set by Nature to their imaginations."[21]

5

The Organic Theory

In explicating what might be called the "naturalist" or "instinctive" theory of the origin of the state, and virtually echoing the position taken on the matter by Cicero (see Chapter 2), Johann K. Bluntschli suggests that the one common cause of the emergence of states, as distinct from the variety of forms in which they appear, is to be found in human nature, "which besides its individual diversity has in it the tendencies of community and unity. These tendencies are developed, and peoples feel themselves to be nations, and seek a corresponding outward form. Thus the inward impulse to Society (*Staatstrieb*) produces external organisation of common life in the form of manly self-government, that is, in the form of the State."[1] The idea that the state is rooted in man's intrinsic nature was also argued in the last century by Adolf Lasson, who wrote: "The external ground for the existence of the State is the nature of man. There are no men without continuity of social life. There is no continuity of social life without order. There is no order without law. There is no law without coercive force. There is no coercive force without organization. And this organization is the State."[2]

This explanation of the origin of the state as a natural phenomenon, which bears some resemblance to aspects of divine and patriarchal theory, implies that the state is an entity that emerges quite independently of the autonomous will of man. Since the state is not created by him, there is little need to justify its existence in his eyes. As a result, the naturalist conception of the state is taken by some of its advocates as a fundamental argument against the idea that the legitimacy of the state is somehow conferred on it by man as a conscious act of acknowledgment. In this view, the state exists because it is part of the natural order of things and not the arbitrary contrivance of man.

Closely allied to this conception of the state is another which sees the state essentially as a self-sustaining "organism" with its own intrinsic purposes and ends, which may be quite different from those of the individuals who constitute its members. This view comports well with the general approach taken by the Greek philosophers, who tended to consider political authority to be a metaphysical necessity arising from the social life of man. The organic theory argues that the state is the inevitable consequence of the needs of human nature and is not an artifact to be made or unmade at will by man. It asserts that the unity of the state, once realized, is inviolable: The members of the state can no more leave it and survive than a limb can exist independent of the body as a whole. The life and well-being of the part is thus bound up with and subordinate to the well-being of the whole. This concept is articulated quite explicitly by Plato.

Our aim in founding the State was not the disproportionate happiness of any one class, but the greatest happiness of the whole; we thought that in a State which is ordered with a view to the good of the whole we should be most likely to find justice, and in the ill-ordered State injustice; and having found them, we might decide which of the two is the happier. . . . And therefore we must consider whether in appointing our guardians we would look to their greatest happiness individually or whether this principle of happiness does not reside in the State as a whole. But if the latter be the truth, then the guardians and auxiliaries, and all others equally with them, must be compelled or induced to do their own work in the best way. And thus the whole State will grow up in a noble order, and the several classes will receive the proportion of happiness which nature assigns to them.[3]

Plato may thus be seen as suggesting that the happiness or well-being of the state is not necessarily the same as the aggregated happiness of its individual members. Indeed, it would appear to matter little if it was not; it is the whole that is most important, and not its component elements. This position was also reflected by Aristotle who, in addition to describing the state in a manner consistent with patriarchal theory (See Chapter 4), also spoke of it as an organism. Thus, after explaining that the individual and the family are prior to the state in the order of time, Aristotle argues that "the polis is prior in the order of nature to the family and the individual. The reason for this is that the whole is necessarily prior [in nature] to the part." He explains that if the body as a whole were to cease to function, were to die, none of its arms or feet would survive in anything but the sense that they would still be called by the same name but would not have the same vital meaning. "Not being self-sufficient when they are isolated, all individuals are so many parts all equally depending on the whole [which alone can bring about self-sufficiency]. The man who is isolated—who is unable to share in the benefits of political association, or has no need to share because he is already self-sufficient—is no part of the polis, and must be either a beast or a god."[4]

After Aristotle, the organic theory seemed to go into eclipse until the dawn of the modern era. Although he does not discuss the matter systematically or in any depth, Niccolò Machiavelli evidently was the first modern theorist of politics to maintain a naturalistic and organic conception of the state, seeing it as an organic structure whose ends transcend those of its component parts. For him the state is a living organism, a "mixed body" composed of individuals, that follows the life cycle typical of other organisms from birth to death.[5] In one particularly significant passage, Machiavelli writes:

There is nothing more true than that all the things of this world have a limit to their existence; but those only run the entire course

ordained for them by Heaven that do not allow their body to
become disorganized, but keep it unchanged in the manner ordained, or if they change it, so do it that it shall be for their
advantage, and not to their injury. And as I speak here of mixed
bodies, such as republics or religious sects, I say that those changes
are beneficial that bring them back to their original principles. And
those are the best-constituted bodies, and have the longest existence, which possess the intrinsic means of frequently renewing
themselves, or such as obtain this renovation in consequence of
some extrinsic accidents. And it is a truth clearer than light that,
without such renovation, these bodies cannot continue to exist;
and the means of renewing them is to bring them back to their
original principles. For, as all religious republics and monarchies
must have within them some goodness, by means of which they
obtain their first growth and reputation, and as in the process of
time this goodness becomes corrupted, it will of necessity destroy
the body unless something intervenes to bring it back to its normal
condition. Thus, the doctors of medicine say, in speaking of the
human body, that 'every day some ill humours gather which must
be cured.' "[6]

It is clear from this remarkable passage that, for Machiavelli, the state's primary interest is not with the well-being
of its individual component elements, which play a secondary
role in its life at best. Its foremost concern is with its own
survival as a political organism, to which everything else must
necessarily be subordinated. The notion of the state taking
risks for causes that transcend its own welfare and interests
is totally alien to Machiavelli, who would probably consider
such a state in dire need of therapeutic care by a "political
doctor." Accordingly, Bluntschli characterized Machiavelli's
view of the state as fundamentally utilitarian: "Public law is
to him only a means to further the welfare of the State, and
to secure the growth of its power. His ideal is exclusively
filled and determined by politics. The State is for him neither
a moral nor a legal (*Rechtwesen*), but only a political being.
Thus, the only standard of all state-acts is utility. What the
power and authority of the State demand, that must the
statesman do, undisturbed by moral and legal considerations. What is hurtful to the welfare of the State he must
avoid."[7]

Perhaps the most prominent modern exponent of the organic theory is Hegel, who considered the state as a *moral* organism, as the earthly embodiment of the ideal ordering of the universe. Hegel specifically points out that he is not at all concerned with the actual origins of the state, either generally or with regard to any particular state. His focus is exclusively on the idea of the state, which is itself "the actuality of the ethical Idea."[8] Warming to his subject, Hegel declares: "The march of God in the world, that is what the state is. The basis of the state is the power of reason actualizing itself as will." His idealization of the state did not extend to the externals of actually existing states, but only to their essence. He was under no illusions about the character of such states. Thus, he observed: "The state is no ideal work of art; it stands on earth and so in the sphere of caprice, chance, and error, and bad behaviour may disfigure it in many respects. But the ugliest of men, or a criminal, or an invalid, or a cripple, is still always a living man. The affirmative, life, subsists despite his defects, and it is this affirmative factor which is our theme here."[9]

The state, according to Hegel, "is an organism," which is itself "the constitution of the state; it is produced perpetually by the state, while it is through it that the state maintains itself." Moreover, the state must be a unity, that is, it cannot survive as an organism if its constituent members free themselves from it. "The nature of an organism is such that unless each of its parts is brought into identity with the others, unless each of them is prevented from achieving autonomy, the whole must perish." As far as Hegel is concerned, all attempts to describe the state by virtue of reciting its characteristics are doomed to failure. The only way the state can be properly understood is by apprehending it as an organism. "One might as well try to understand the nature of God by listing his attributes, while the truth is that we must intuit God's life in that life itself."[10]

The organic view was clearly reflected in more recent times by Jacques Maritain who in discussing the question of political authority, drew a sharp distinction between the "democracy of the individual" or "Anarchic Democracy," which he saw as contrary to the natural order of things, and the "democracy of the person" or "Organic Democracy," which he advocated. "The necessity of authority in the political community, as of the necessity of the State itself, is inscribed in the very nature of things. The political community having, in so far as it is a whole, its own reality, its own unity, and its own life, is by this very fact superior to its parts as such, and demands a hierarchic distribution of its organs." Accordingly, reason demands that certain central organs, whose functions relate to the well-being of the whole, should possess an authority over the others. This is evident since we live in an imperfect world, continually subjected to contingencies, where objective considerations alone will not produce the desired agreement of numerous individual minds with regard to what needs to be done for the general welfare of the state and its constituents. "Even if all individuals possessed perfect reason and perfect rectitude of will, the unified conduct of social affairs would still require a political authority and a hierarchy.... Organic democracy does not suppress, even in principle, either authority or power. It wishes both to come from the people and to be exercised in its name."[11] Although Maritain categorically rejects as illegitimate any regime that rules in its own interest rather than in the interest of the common good, in his organic democracy the people do not actually govern in any significant sense.

From the standpoint of organic theory, the definition of the state would necessarily contain at least one element that we omitted from the discussion in Chapter 1. As pointed out by T. W. Weldon, according to organic theory, "an independent community organized as government and governed and supreme within a defined geographical area constitutes a genuine individual or person and is known as the State."[12] Considered from a juridical perspective, the terms "individual" and "person" employed in this definition are not intended as metaphors; the state is considered to be an actual person and not merely analogous to one. Bluntschli, perhaps one of the most articulate and expansive advocates of organic theory, notes that we define a person, in private law, as a being to whom we can ascribe a legal will (*Rechtswille*); one who can acquire, create, and possess rights. He argues that this concept is of equal significance in the realm of public law. "The State is *par excellence* a person in the sense of public law (*öffentlich-rechtliche Person*). The purpose of the whole constitution is to enable the person of the State to express and realise its will (*Staatswille*), which is different from the individual wills of all individuals, and different from the sum of them."[13]

A similar position was held by Heinrich von Treitschke, even though he believed the state actually came into existence in the first place through an act of imposition of will by an individual or a group rather than by natural means. Nonetheless, he asserted that, once it is brought into being, "the State has a personality, primarily in the juridical, and secondly in the politico-moral sense." In this regard, he considered the state as being no different in principle from an individual. He observed that every individual who is able to exercise his will in law is considered as having a legal personality, and it is quite evident that the state possesses such an ability. Indeed, Treitschke argues that the legal personality of the state is more complete and surpasses that of the individual. "In State treaties it is the will of the State which is expressed, not the personal desires of the individuals who conclude them ... The state, then, has from all time been a legal person. It appears to be so still more clearly in the historico-moral sense. States must be conceived as the great collective personalities of history, thoroughly capable of bearing responsibility and blame."[14]

However, although Treitschke's views clearly reflect the perspectives of organic theory, he strongly objects to the description of the state as an "organism." He considers it quite misleading to speak of it in this manner. Treitschke acknowledges that the characterization of the state as an organism may have been justified at one time as a means of drawing a sharp distinction from the conception of the state as an instrument or mechanism for serving the popular will. It thus became customary to speak of the state as an organism to emphasize its natural rather than conventional origins. But, he warns, in consideration of much of the criticism that is levied against organic theory, "it is dangerous to import the terminology of one science into another. . . . Above all, the phrase does not in any sense express the nature of the State. There are countless organisms without conscious will, but will is the State's essence."[15]

Treitschke's views on the organic character of the state are also seconded in the writings of Ernest Barker, who stated: "The application of the category of organism to the State is necessary and valuable. It is necessary, because it gives a true idea of the kind of unity which exists in the State: it is valuable, because it is an antidote to false ideas of the unity of the State as legal in its essence and contractual in its form." Barker sees the contractual conception of the state as degrading it into a business transaction from which one may withdraw when it no longer suits his individual purposes. The organic conception of the state serves as a corrective to this misconception. "It teaches that the unity of the State is not one made by hands, and by hands to be broken, but an inevitable outcome of human nature and human needs." As such, the State is a vital body from which its members cannot simply decide to dissociate. This reality causes individual citizens to become linked to one another just as each is connected to the whole, establishing mutual concerns and interests that transcend those of any single member. "The conception of a common weal and a vital union supersedes that of self-interest and a causal nexus."[16]

Nonetheless, like Treitschke, Barker is disturbed by the use of the term "organism" to describe the state. He notes that an organism has certain basic characteristics: It is a vital structure composed of elements that are different in kind; it contains diverse elements that are complementary to one another and are mutually dependent; the health of the organism depends on the proper functioning of each component element; and, as a living structure, the organism is capable of a growth from within that affects all of its constituent elements simultaneously. But, Barker says, while all of these may apply to the state as well, the notion of "organism" may only be applied to the state metaphorically. "The State," he insists, "is not an organism; but it is like an organism. It is not an organism, because it is not a physical structure. It is a mental structure—a union of different minds in a common purpose." The state is analogous to an organism in that the achievement of its purposes is dependent upon the proper discharge of their functions by its component members, and that its growth and development come from within, affecting all its elements at the same time. "The fact, however, remains, that the State is not an organism, because it is a self-determining system of minds which are themselves self-determining; and the whole analogy leads to confusion instead of clearness, unless we are clear about the terms of the comparison, and unless we are also clear that metaphor is not argument, and that a parallel between the State and the individual is not an explanation of their relation."[17]

Even though organic theorists apparently think of the state as a sociological phenomenon, and are sensitive to the risks of misunderstanding that may result from describing the state as an organism, they nonetheless tend to prefer describing it as a vital organism rather than as a lifeless abstraction. Their semantic problem is to find a means of adequately describing the state as something more than the aggregate of its parts. Bluntschli, for one, illustrates what he means by referring to the state as an organism by comparing it with a work of art. "An oil painting," he says, "is something other than a mere aggregation of drops of oil and colour, a statue is something other than a combination of marble particles, a man is not a mere quantity of cells and blood corpuscles; and so too the nation is not a mere sum of citizens, and the State is not a mere collection of external regulations." He freely admits that the state is not a direct product of nature and therefore not a true organism. But, he insists, it is only indirectly the creation of man. "The tendency to political life is to be found in human nature, and so far the State has a natural basis; but the realisation of this political tendency has been left to human labour, and human arrangement, and so far the State is a product of human activity, and its organism is a copy of a natural organism."[18]

Accordingly, when Bluntschli speaks of the state as an organism, he clearly does not intend that the term be understood in a strict biological sense. The use of the term reflects his interest in certain characteristics of natural organisms that he sees replicated in the state. For one thing, every such organism is a union of material elements and vital forces. Although an organism is and remains a totality, its component parts have elements which are animated by special drives and capacities that serve, in a variety of ways, to satisfy the needs of the organism as a whole. Finally, the organism develops from within but grows externally. Bluntschli sees all these elements as evident in the organic nature of the state. "In the State spirit and body, will and active organs are necessarily bound together in one life. The one national spirit, which is something different from the average sum of the contemporary spirit of all citizens, is the spirit of the State; the one national will, which is different from the average will of the multitude, is the will of the State."[19]

From the standpoint of organic theory, the constitution of the state represents the body of the political organism. It contains specialized organs that represent the state and reflect its will in a regime of law. It establishes a head who governs, courts for the public dispensation of justice, a wide variety of institutions to provide for the intellectual and material interests of the community, and an army to assure the public interest through organized force, as appropriate. Actual individual states, of course, will differ from one another, just as individual persons do, in terms of spirit, character, and form. But they will all share certain common constitutional characteristics.

Every office and every political assembly provided for by the constitution of the state is considered to be a unique member of the political organism, each having its own special purpose and function. By contrast with the mechanistic view of the state, which considers the offices of the state as mere mechanisms with established and essentially invariable procedures and patterns of activity, Bluntschli conceives the offices of the state as having an intrinsically spiritual character. This enables them to adapt to the exigencies of time and place, deviating from established patterns to meet the special demands imposed by particular circumstances. Each office or arm of the state, therefore, has an inherent ability to influence and shape the character of the officeholder by virtue of the different roles he is called upon to perform. For example, the office of judge is held in such awe and esteem that it has the capacity to affect the character of the person appointed to it. The assignment of a weak person to the post will likely result in his becoming ennobled by it, inspiring in him a determination to fulfill the expectations of the office to the maximum possible extent. Such a transformation of personality may not be lasting in every respect, but every individual exposed to such an experience of office will retain some aspects of its influence. Bluntschli suggests that if the official is impressionable, he will acknowledge that the office itself has an intrinsic soul which establishes a close and immediate connection with his own individuality. On the other hand, where an office becomes lifeless and sinks into unthinking and uncreative routine, it becomes self-defeating and even counterproductive. Similarly, when the state itself becomes transformed into a mere instrument, its ultimate collapse becomes inevitable.

Bluntschli argues that nations and states follow their own general patterns of growth and decay. The political history of a nation or state clearly extends beyond the life spans of its individual members. Like a person, every state passes through several stages of development, each of which has its own special character. The state will therefore be quite different in its youth than when it reaches maturity, and the competent statesman will constantly adjust his thinking and approaches to the particular stage of development or decay in which his state happens to be at a particular point in time. It is in this respect that the state most clearly differs from the natural organism. Biological organisms—plants, animals, and men—grow and decay in regular periods and stages, but the life cycle of states and political institutions seems to be quite irregular. Their normal patterns of growth and decline may be affected dramatically by aberrations produced by the unpredictable behavior of individuals as well as by external contingencies. Bluntschli insists, nonetheless, that these deviations from the norm are neither sufficiently numerous nor of sufficient historical importance to invalidate the general proposition. On the contrary, in his view, they are much rarer and generally much less significant than imagined by those impressionable people whose opinions are determined by the immediacy of contemporary events. We learn from history that while the state is an organism, it is one of a higher and special order. It has moral character and spiritual qualities; it is capable of absorbing the emotions and thoughts of the nation, and of giving expression to them in laws and actions. According to Bluntschli,

History ascribes to the State a personality which, having spirit and body, possesses and manifests a will of its own. The glory and honour of the State have always elevated the heart of its sons, and animated them to sacrifices. For freedom and independence, for the rights of the State, the noblest and best have in all times and in all nations expended their goods and their lives. To extend the reputation and the power of the State, to further its welfare and its happiness, has universally been regarded as one of the most honourable duties of gifted men. The joys and sorrows of the State have always been shared by all its citizens. The whole great idea of Fatherland and love of country would be inconceivable if the State did not possess this high moral and personal character.[20]

Given this perspective, it is not surprising that the organic theory of the state was adopted as the basis of the modern doctrines of fascism and totalitarianism. According to Alfredo Rocco, one of the principal ideologists of fascism, "Society is not, as it appears in the political philosophy taught by demo-liberals, a mere sum of individuals which can be resolved into its separate elements, but is a real organism with an existence and a purpose quite distinct from those of its particular members." Rocco sees unrelenting conflict as the "basic law of life of all social organisms, as it is of all biological ones; societies are formed, gain strength and move forward through conflict." Accordingly, the state too is subject to this ineluctable law of the struggle for existence, in which survival is the highest value. Unrelenting struggle "is thus the necessary historical form of the life of society, which is of indefinite length, as distinct from the ephemeral value of the individual."[21] Or, as articulated by Benito Mussolini: "Fascism reaffirms the State as the true reality of the individual. . . . Therefore, for the Fascist, everything is in the State, and nothing human or spiritual exists, much less has value, outside the State. In this sense Fascism is totalitarian, and the Fascist State, the synthesis and unity of all values, interprets, develops and gives strength to the whole life of the people."[22]

Critics of the organic theory have argued that even the analogy drawn between the state and the natural organism does not hold. In the case of a true organism, such as the human being, it is evident that its component elements exist solely to support and perpetuate the life of the whole. The individual members of the body have no independent existence and are incapable of autonomous acts of will. Moreover, the human organism tends, by virtue of its central nervous system, to extend and intensify the influence and control of the whole over the action of its parts. These conditions do not obtain in the state, not even in the totalitarian state, even though it may aspire to achieve such centrality in the lives of its members. To the extent that the state strives to achieve its intrinsic purposes, it surely provides ever greater security and tranquility for the individual and, at least in open democratic societies, assures him a continually expanding private sphere of action within which he is increasingly less constrained in his behavior.

Furthermore, there is a vast difference between the individual and the state with respect to morphological constraints on growth and development. For the living human organism, the limitations on its capacities for assimilation and organic increase are quite rigidly fixed. For the state, on the other hand, the situation is rather different. Although the form and development of the state are certainly subject to the influences and constraints placed on it by the laws of nature and other objective factors, it still possesses capacities for growth and fundamental change that far transcend anything that could be predicated of a natural organism such as man. As suggested by Willoughby, the State, "of its own will may change its form to an extent to which no theoretical limit can be placed."[23] Finally, some critics of the organic theory also argue that it is a misuse of language to speak of the state even as a "moral organism." Although one may attribute moral personality to the state, that does not make it a person in the commonsense meaning of the term. Since morality is an attribute of a real person, and not of a thing, it is simply improper to apply such a concept to the state.

In sum, the naturalist explanation of the origin of the state really explains very little. The assertion that political authority is natural is not an adequate response to the fundamental questions that spurred the inquiry into origins in the first place. While it may serve as a possible justification for the continuing existence or even exaltation of the state, it does not tell us how the state came into being. It does not explain the means by which "the inward impulse to Society" is transformed into an empirical state. Although our common experience would seem to corroborate Aristotle's assertion that man is by nature an animal intended to live in a polis, the evidence for this is still quite inconclusive. There is no sound basis for dismissing those individuals who deny that they feel any natural or instinctive urge toward sociability as aberrations. The case for the state as a universal natural necessity that will satisfy their objections still remains to be made. Finally, the explanatory power of the organic theory is deficient because it says nothing about in whose hands the natural authority of the state should be vested or how that vesting takes place.

6

The Force Theory

In contrast to the theories discussed earlier, all of which, in
one way or another, considered the state to be rooted in the
nature of the universe, the force theory maintains that the
state is the deliberate creation of man. It is considered to
have its roots in nature only to the extent that the state
emerges as a direct consequence of man's aggressive and
egocentric instincts and behavior. An early exponent of the
force theory is the thirteenth-century Muslim thinker Ibn
Jama'a. In his *Tahrir al-Ahkam*, he argued that the state
emerges when a man of authority, by force of arms, subdues
a people and brings them under his control. This, in his
opinion, was a consequence of the inability of men to join
spontaneously to organize their political life. Thus, it became
necessary for a strong leader to arise and impose his will,
leading to the development of the political society and the
early form of the state.[1]

A similar view was expounded in the fourteenth century
by Ibn Khaldun, who suggested that while society is natural
to man, there is an evident need for a restraining force within
society to keep people from attacking each other. He considered this predatory behavior to be a consequence of man's

innate animal propensities for aggressiveness and oppression
of his fellow men. Even though man develops weapons that
permit him to protect himself from the beasts of the field,
these are of little avail against other men because each can
make equal use of such devices. As a result, it becomes
necessary that restraints on human behavior be imposed by
a central sovereign, who wields firmly held power and authority, to maintain security and peace in society. Ibn Khaldun suggests that the idea of sovereignty is "peculiar to man,
suited to his nature and indispensable to his existence." He
concludes that "the state is therefore to society as form is
to matter, for the form by its nature preserves the matter
and, as philosophers have shown, the two are inseparable.
For a state is inconceivable without a society; while a society
without a state is well nigh impossible, owing to the aggressive propensities of men, which require a restraint. A polity
therefore arises, either theocratic or kingly, and this is what
we mean by state."[2]

This approach was echoed by the fifteenth century Persian
thinker, Fadl Allah b. Ruzbihan, who wrote in his *Suluk al-
Muluk*: "Man is a political being by nature and in gaining
his livelihood he needs the society of his own kind to co-
operate with him and to be his partners, but since the power
of lust and passion stimulates men to violence and discord,
there must be a just man who will abate violence . . . there
is need of a person singled out by divine support, who is
endowed with ability to manage affairs and with power and
authority so that he is obeyed . . . such a person is the king."[3]

How does one person come to dominate the society? Ibn
Khaldun suggests that the state is based on an extension of
the principle of "social solidarity" which is found only in
groups related by blood ties or by other connections which
create similar bonds. He bases this on the conviction that
blood ties exert an innate force that binds most people so
connected, causing them to be concerned with any injury
inflicted on their relatives.[4] These family groupings coalesce
into a broader societal structure, creating a new sense of
solidarity among themselves. However, the constituent families of the larger society are not all equal, and one "being

more powerful than the rest, dominates and directs the others and finally absorbs them, thus forming an association which ensures victory over other peoples and states." Within that leading family group there is bound to be one outstanding personality that dominates the group. "That person will therefore be appointed as leader of the wider group, because of the domination enjoyed by his house over the others."[5] Ibn Khaldun's approach to the question is consistent with the findings of modern anthropology. Thus, Lucy Mair observes: "In fact those peoples who believe that they are all kin do not have the type of political structure that we call the state. The state itself in its simplest form entails the recognition that *one* body of kin have an exclusive claim to provide the ruler from among themselves."[6]

In sixteenth century Europe the force theory was expounded by Jean Bodin. In setting forth his philosophy of society, Bodin drew a distinction between civil society and the state. With respect to the former, he agreed with Aristotle that all society had its natural origin in the family and that civil society was the natural extension of the social nature of man. However, he attributed a rather different origin to the state. In what amounts to a state of nature, before any form of state structure or commonwealth was known, all authority and power rested with the natural head of the family. He was sovereign in his household and had the power of life and death over his immediate family members. "But force, violence, ambition, avarice, and the passion for vengeance, armed men against one another. The result of the ensuing conflicts was to give victory to some, and to reduce the rest to slavery." Another unforeseen consequence of these struggles was the emergence of a new power structure. The man who had been chosen to be their leader by the victors had achieved such stature from his success that he was able to retain his authority over both the victors and the vanquished. Those who willingly accepted his authority became his loyal and faithful followers, subsequently imposing it by force on the others. "Thus was lost the full and entire liberty of each man to live according to his own free will, without subjection to anyone. It was completely lost to the vanquished and converted into unmitigated servitude; it was qualified in the case of the victors in that they now rendered obedience to a sovereign leader. . . . Reason and common sense alike point to the conclusion that the origin and foundation of commonwealths was in force and violence."[7]

During that same period, this position was also argued by Alonso de Castrillo, in his *Tractado de república*. Rejecting the divine theory of the state, he asserted that all men are created free by nature and that there is no evidence that it was God's intention that one man should rule over another. However, man is characterized by reckless tendencies to seek change and innovation, and thus unintentionally created the opportunity for political authority to be imposed on him by force. Once compelled to obey a superior authority, such obedience was later institutionalized through enactments of positive law. As a result, Castrillo insists, it is an error to maintain that political authority derives from natural law. The truth is that its roots are in violence and forcible subjugation. But, he suggests, "once the world's innocence was corrupted no other way lay open but to obey the monarch if greater evils were to be avoided. It is therefore imperative for the sake of the common weal that the citizens render obedience to the king."[8]

In his criticism of the idea that states and governments were established in the first instance by a voluntary act of the members of society, that is, by a "social contract," David Hume argued, in a statement that has remained a remarkably apt description of the rise of authoritarian states and governments:

Almost all the governments which exist at present, or of which there remains any record in story, have been founded originally either on usurpation or conquest or both, without any pretense of a fair consent or voluntary subjection of the people. When an artful and bold man is placed at the head of an army or faction, it is often easy for him, by employing sometimes violence, sometimes false pretenses, to establish his dominion over a people a hundred times more numerous than his partisans. He allows no such open communication that his enemies can know with certainty their number or force. He gives them no leisure to assemble to-

gether in a body to oppose him. Even all those who are the instruments of his usurpation may wish his fall, but their ignorance
of each other's intention keeps them in awe and is the sole cause
of his security. By such arts as these many governments have been
established, and this is all the original contract which they have to
boast of.[9]

Hume does not deny the possibility that some states may
indeed have emerged through a contractual process, although he thinks it highly improbable. Consequently, he
finds it necessary to postulate a different foundation of political authority. In his view, the more likely reality is that
"the original establishment was formed by violence and submitted to from necessity. The subsequent administration is
also supported by power and acquiesced in by the people
not as a matter of choice but of obligation."[10] This position
is echoed in the statement of Treitschke that "The State is
born in a community whenever a group or an individual has
achieved sovereignty by imposing its will upon the whole
body."[11]

The idea that force is a critical element in the founding of
the state is also accepted by Thomas Holland, who gives it
a normative jurisprudential legitimacy in his definition of the
institution: "A State is a numerous assemblage of human
beings generally occupying a certain territory amongst whom
the will of the majority, or of an ascertainable class of persons, is, by the strength of such a majority or class, made
to prevail against any of their number who oppose it."[12] This
acknowledgment of the role of force in the origin of the state
is given dramatic expression by Friedrich Nietzsche. In discussing the source of the notion of a "bad conscience," he
argues that the only way an amorphous and naturally unrestrained population could be brought to accept the constraints of life under the state was by force; nothing short of
violence and coercion could have brought it about. In his
view, the primeval state was nothing but a horrendous tyranny imposed on man, "a grinding ruthless piece of machinery, which went on working, till this raw material of a
semi-animal populace was not only thoroughly kneaded and

elastic, but also moulded." With regard to his use of the term "state," Nietzsche insists that its meaning is self-evident. It refers to "a race of conquerors and masters, which with all its war-like organisation and all its organising power pounces with its terrible claws on a population, in numbers possibly tremendously superior, but yet formless, as yet nomad. Such is the origin of the 'State.' "[13]

Considerable support for the force theory also comes from modern sociologists. One of the most notable among these is Franz Oppenheimer. "The State," he writes, "completely in its genesis, essentially and almost completely during the first stages of its existence, is a social institution, forced by a victorious group of men on a defeated group, with the sole purpose of regulating the dominion of the victorious group over the vanquished, and securing itself against revolt from within and attacks from abroad." Oppenheimer insists that no primitive state known to history originated in any other manner, regardless of local traditions that may suggest otherwise. The relentless pattern of the past has been of one warlike tribe "breaking through the boundaries of some less warlike people, settling down as nobility and founding its State."[14]

A related formulation of the force theory is the historical-materialist conception of Frederick Engels. In his view, the emergence of the state through force, and its subsequent embodiment and institutionalization of that force, came as a secondary but historically necessary consequence of the level of economic development that characterized early societies. Based on the anthropological studies of Lewis Morgan, Engels concluded that, as the primitive natural families became increasingly extended, they tended to organize themselves in larger kinship groups, or gentes. Subsequently, groups of such gens were formed into still more extensive kinship groups or tribes. "The members of the gens owed each other help, protection, and especially assistance in avenging injury by strangers. The individual looked for his security to the protection of the gens, and could rely upon receiving it; to wrong him was to wrong his whole gens."[15] Each gens had a similar set of traditions of self-governance which were reflected in the structure of its regime. The unwritten gentile constitution provided for a council: "the democratic assembly of all male and female adult gentiles, all with equal votes. This council elected *sachems* (leaders in peace time), war-chiefs . . . and deposed them; it took decisions regarding blood revenge or payment of atonement for murdered gentiles; it adopted strangers into the gens. In short, it was the sovereign power in the gens."[16]

Engels waxed rhapsodic about the structure and functioning of the primitive gens and its constitution. "And what a wonderful constitution it is, this gentile constitution, in all its childlike simplicity! No soldiers, no gendarmes or police, no nobles, regents, prefects, or judges, no prisons, no lawsuits—and everything takes its orderly course. All quarrels and disputes are settled by the whole of the community affected."[17] However, this idyllic situation was destined to come to an end with the emergence of the institution of private property, and the changes that it brought in the character of the community. The gentile constitution was predicated on two key considerations. It presupposed an extremely undeveloped state of production, and it was based on the matriarchal principle which, by requiring marriage outside the gens, had the effect of promoting equality within. The natural consequence of these factors was that it was impracticable to have any concentration of population. Instead, the gens typically had its members dispersed in small groups over a wide area. Under these primitive conditions, "man was bounded by his tribe, both in relation to strangers from outside the tribe and to himself; the tribe, the gens, and their institutions were sacred and inviolable, a higher power established by nature, to which the individual subjected himself unconditionally in feeling, thought, and action."[18]

Over time, according to Engels, presumably as man developed improved means and methods of production, economic conditions changed and men began to progress beyond mere subsistence. And, as greater productivity created incentives for the acquisition of property, the gentile constitution began to disintegrate, bringing about fundamental changes in the structure of the gens. The matriarchal basis of the gens was discarded, and "Father-right, with transmission of the property to the children, by which accumulation of wealth within the family was favored and the family itself became a power as against the gens." The effects of the new inequality of wealth on the constitution were dramatic. The first signs of the emergence of a hereditary nobility and monarchy were to be seen. Slavery, which at first was a condition imposed only on prisoners of war, now began to be extended to fellow-members of the tribe and even the gens itself. The traditional intertribal wars degenerated into systematic pillage for the purpose of acquiring slaves, cattle, and booty, and became a regular source of wealth for the more powerful. Violence and disorder increased as wealth became the highest value in society. "Only one thing was wanting: an institution which not only secured the newly acquired riches of individuals against the communistic traditions of the gentile order, which not only sanctified the private property formerly so little valued . . . [but an institution which] perpetuated not only this growing cleavage of society into classes, but also the right of the possessing class to exploit the non-possessing, and the rule of the former over the latter. And this institution came. The *state* was invented."[19]

The primary purpose of the state, in this view, is to consolidate the existing class divisions of the society and thereby to ensure the security of the property of the dominant class. Engels thus rejects the notion that the state is fundamentally an external imposition. It is rather an imposition from within which becomes necessary at a particular stage in societal development. The state, in effect, represents the admission that the society is afflicted by irreconcilable antagonisms that it is incapable of mediating. Consequently, to assure that these antagonisms do not "consume themselves and society in fruitless struggle, a power, apparently standing above society, has become necessary to moderate the conflict and keep it within the bounds of 'order'; and this power, arisen out of society, but placing itself above it and increasingly alienating itself from it, is the state."[20] But this state is normally dominated by the most powerful economic class, which uses its economic power to become the political ruling class as well. In this way it acquires additional means of suppressing and exploiting the weaker economic class.[21] Engels concludes his argument by asserting that "the state, therefore, has not existed from all eternity. There have been societies which have managed without it, which had no notion of the state or state power. At a definite stage of economic development, which necessarily involved the cleavage of society into classes, the state became a necessity because of this cleavage."[22]

The implication drawn from this scenario by Engels was that, once the existence of classes became an impediment to the development of more advanced modes of economic development and production, the state would lose its purpose and eventually would be discarded as an anachronism. With the elimination of the classes it was intended to differentiate, its fundamentally repressive character changes. As the state becomes more truly representative of society as a whole, it makes itself increasingly superfluous. "As soon as there is no longer any class of society to be held in subjection; as soon as, along with class domination and the struggle for individual existence based on the former anarchy of production, the collisions and excesses arising from these have also been abolished, there is nothing more to be repressed, and a special repressive force, a state, is no longer necessary." At this final stage in the history of the state, "government over persons is replaced by the administration of things and the direction of the processes of production. The state is not 'abolished,' it withers away."[23]

Engels's argument was adopted in its entirety by V. I. Lenin who considered it as "the basic idea of Marxism on the question of the historical role and meaning of the state. The state is the product and the manifestation of the irreconcilability of class antagonisms. The state arises when, where, and to the extent that the class antagonisms cannot be objectively reconciled. . . . The state is an organ of domination of a definite class which cannot be reconciled with its antipode." Lenin, however, went beyond Engels's text

and drew a revolutionary rather than an evolutionary conclusion. Making the implicit assumption that it is contrary
to human experience, if not human nature, to yield power
voluntarily, he held the view that the ruling class would
continue to wield the oppressive power of the state even
after its reason for existence was eliminated. "If the state is
the product of the irreconcilable character of class antagonisms, if it is a force standing above society and 'increasingly
separating from it,' [as Engels stipulated,] then it is clear
that the liberation of the oppressed class is impossible not
only without a violent revolution, but also without the destruction of the apparatus of state power, which was created
by the ruling class and in which this 'separation' is embodied."[24]

Notwithstanding these extreme formulations of the force
theory, the essential class basis of the state is also acknowledged by writers such as Robert M. MacIver. In considering
the development of early societies, he observed that as social
life became increasingly complex, there was a tendency for
the primitive and more democratic rule of custom and tradition to yield to a new social and political order involving
a far greater degree of subordination and control in the name
of the whole. This provided the occasion for the state to take
on a new dimension. As it became more essential to the
maintenance of the social order, it also became more asser-
tive and restrictive. "The state becomes identified with a
privileged class. It stands for dominance and obedience . . .
The state becomes the embodiment of power, but only in
proportion as it becomes the instrument of a class, only as
it is identified with a privileged order."[25]

Critics of the force theory dispute the notion that might,
as such, can be understood to constitute a natural basis for
the state and its authority. It is argued that there can be no
causal connection between might and right. As noted by
William Samuel Lilly, "no doubt force is an essential element
in every regimen. But it is curious that any thoughtful person
should have found in it the sufficient explanation of government. Every polity, however rude, requires the ideas of right,

and of law for the maintenance of right. Might, without these ideas, would not give rise to a commonwealth, but to a gang of robbers; to anarchy plus the sword."[26] Indeed, Jean-Jacques Rousseau reminds us that the moral obligation of obedience to authority can have reference only to a person endowed with unconstrained freedom of will and action. Where physical compulsion is involved, he asserts, "I fail to see what moral effect it can have. To yield to force is an act of necessity, not of will, at the most, an act of prudence. In what sense can it be a duty?" It is evident that if one must obey in deference to force, or the threat of force, the notion of simultaneously acting from duty is quite superfluous. Under such circumstances, where obedience is compelled, no one is morally obligated to obey. Force cannot create a moral foundation for state authority, nor can it impose a moral obligation of obedience. Rousseau argues that in such a case it is pointless to assert, "Obey the powers that be. If this means yield to force, it is a good precept, but superfluous; I can answer for its never being violated."[27]

Croce, however, cautions that we should not restrict the idea of force exclusively to that of the application of physical strength. Instead, "we must think of force in the complete truth of all human and spiritual force, which includes the wisdom of the intellect no less than the strength of the arm." With force understood in this broader sense, he argues that it is evident that the exercise of force cannot be limited to only a few individuals within any particular society. He considers the significant aspect of force to be not its quantitative but rather its qualitative distribution. There are numerous people within any society who are thus capable of exerting pressure on others in light of their attitudes, abilities, and virtues. "Each one of these seeks its complement in the others, each one needs the others, each one can in reciprocal fashion impose itself upon the others, threaten to deprive them of its own support, or, as we say, exert pressure on the others. And the result of these different pressures is the agreement on a way of living, the reciprocal accord."[28] In other words, whoever possesses the power to persuade must be considered as a force in society.

As noted at the beginning of this chapter, the force theory, which considers the state as an artifact created by man, represents a fundamental departure from those theories which regard the state as a natural or divine phenomenon. However, the force theory also faces a radical challenge from the consent theories of the state, which also regard it as an artificial construct created by man. As we turn now to a consideration of the consent theories of the genesis of the state, it will be useful to bear in mind Croce's observation that, "in the field of politics, force and consent are correlative terms, and one does not exist without the other. . . . every consent is more or less forced; that is, every consent is based on the 'force' of certain facts and is therefore 'conditioned.' "[29]

7

The Consent Theory (I)

By contrast with force theory, the consent theory postulates the origin of the state in the voluntary agreement of its members. The consent theory thus predicates the state on an original pact entered into by the individuals of a society, who, prior to that time, had been entirely independent of any central political control. If we make the assumption that these individuals possessed an inherent right of self-determination, then it would appear that the only way a central authority that places constraints on their freedom of action can be justified is by its somehow having previously received their consent to the imposition of such controls over them. Since it is based on the obvious assumption that the individual is naturally endowed with autonomous rights, the appeal of the consent theory to modern sensibilities has been such as to make it a major topic of political speculation and study to this day. It should be borne in mind from the outset, however, that the consent theory is not necessarily an ally of liberal democratic thought. In fact, it has also been used to justify conservative and even reactionary political views.

With regard to the latter, in an attempt to vindicate the principle of the natural inequality of men, a half century ago

Charles Maurras, perhaps the preeminent spokesman for the French right, invoked the idea of the social contract in support of his effort, even as he lamented the theory's loss of contemporary significance because of what he considered the corrupting influence of liberal democratic ideas. He argued that, as the prototypical individual progresses from adolescence to adulthood, "an irrepressible wave of initial confidence makes him desire and solicit of his fellow man help and collaboration of the two together. But at this point, an instinct no less forceful generates the reverse movement, a wave of mistrust which impels him to desire and solicit guarantees and precautions to control the use of that help and collaboration." Man begins to search for a means of assuring his security on a durable basis, and determines that this may best be achieved by concluding an agreement to such effect with his fellowmen. "Whether such a contract is sworn or not, by the spoken word or not, whether written on brick, stone, hide, bark or paper, it will be in terms of the mutual faith in one another of persons who at last decide to commit their free wills according to the light of the fully awakened, fully conscious spirit of each."

Maurras observes that man's placement of his faith in the benefits to be achieved from such association should come as no surprise to us, since it derives from a common sense of weakness and the need for support and assistance in the ongoing struggle for existence. What man hopes to achieve by his entering into this association is that which he cannot do for himself. And it is for this reason that Maurras sees the idea of the natural inequality of man rooted in the very concept of the social contract. He asserts that what drives man to enter into such an agreement is precisely to gain the support of others who are unlike himself, who can compensate for his weaknesses rather than merely duplicate them. "What he wanted in others was what he could not quite find in himself." Of course, the mere assertion of this does not make it so. One can just as easily make the opposite argument, that man seeks to join in association with his equals, because this permits him to multiply his strengths to the mutual benefit of all. Nonetheless, what is of particular interest here is Maurras's view of the importance of the social contract as the basis for political society and the state. "To live we must associate. To live well we must contract. . . . Bound and sealed by contract, association is justly regarded as the greatest miracle of that chemical synthesis of which human nature is capable."[1]

It remains to be seen, however, whether the consent theory—or the contract theory, as it is commonly referred to—in one form or another can provide an adequate account of the emergence of the state as we know it.

The notion of contract, as it is employed in political theory, carries a double meaning. First, it is used to describe an agreement between the rulers and the ruled, according to which political authority is vested in particular hands. The purpose of such an agreement is to establish the legitimacy of a government, existing or prospective, in the exercise of political power. For purposes of the following discussion, this type of agreement may be categorized as a "governmental compact." It should be noted that this kind of agreement presupposes the prior existence of an organized political society. As observed by Ernest Barker, "The theory of a contract of government really postulates, as a prior condition, the theory of a contract of society. There must already be something in the nature of an organized community . . . before there can be any contract between ruler and subjects."[2] Accordingly, the term is also used to describe an agreement between individuals in a particular community to establish a political society, without necessarily specifying in the original agreement in whom political authority is to be vested or how it is to be exercised. Such an agreement would merely account for the origin of the state in general without regard to its specific form. This type of agreement is generally referred to as the "Social contract," but might more properly be called the "Political contract," since it is supposed to create an organized political society where none existed previously.

The notion of a primeval social contract finds early expression in Plato's *Republic*, where Glaucon presents his view of the origin and nature of justice. "They say that to do injustice is, by nature, good; to suffer injustice, evil; but that the evil is greater than the good. And so when men have both done and suffered injustice and have had experience of both, not being able to avoid the one and obtain the other, they think that they had better agree among themselves to have neither; hence there arise laws and mutual covenants."[3] Although similar intimations of the idea appeared in later Greek philosophic thought as well, the concept of a social contract as such did not emerge as a prominent issue in western political theory for another two millennia. Far greater attention was given to the parallel notion of the governmental compact, which was more immediately relevant to the always troublesome question of the legitimacy of existing states and political regimes.

In antiquity, the contract idea, both social and governmental, appears to have been given greater attention in the East than in the West. We already noted the articulation of these concepts in the *Mahabharata*, in connection with the discussion of the divine theory in Chapter 3. There is also a clear intimation of the consent theory in the *Arthasastra* of Kautilya, where he sets forth the following concept of the genesis of the state: "People suffering from anarchy, as illustrated by the proverbial tendency of a large fish swallowing a small one, first elected Manu, the Vaivasvata, to be their king; and allotted one-sixth of the grains grown and one-tenth of merchandise as sovereign dues. Fed by this payment, kings took upon themselves the responsibility of maintaining the safety and security of their subjects, and of being answerable for the sins of their subjects when the principle of levying just punishments and taxes has been violated."[4] By stating that it is the people who elect the king, Kautilya would appear to be suggesting that they must already be constituted in a society that would enable them to carry out such an electoral process. Moreover, he also indicates that the king is "answerable" for political abuses, further suggesting, at least implicitly, the existence of a governmental compact as well.

Similarly, the discussion of the idea of a primeval social contract, followed by a governmental compact, to be found in the *Digha Nikaya*, the Pali canon of early Buddhism, is of particular interest and relevance. In that work, the Buddha purportedly explains to his disciples the evolution of man and his institutions. His dissertation on the subject is presented within the context of Buddhist ideas concerning the cosmic law of periodic dissolution and reconstitution of the universe.

According to this conception, during the process of rebirth of the world human beings ultimately reemerge with the same essential qualities they possessed earlier as they feed upon the high-quality, self-ripening rice that appears on the earth to sustain them. However, men are not content with their mere subsistence on the bounty provided by nature, and desire to acquire more than they need. Surrendering to their lust, humans begin to accumulate and store surplus quantities of the staple, thereby giving rise to the notion of property. This avarice soon leads to serious shortages of the life-sustaining rice, precipitating a crisis which is only resolved by the people gathering together and deciding to divide and demarcate their rice fields. Inevitably, there emerges an individual who is too greedy to be satisfied with his own rice field and proceeds to make use of his neighbor's as well. The other field owners cannot accept this situation and arrest and censure him for his act, making him promise not to repeat it. When he does do it again he is physically attacked by the others. These incidents exemplify the four evils of theft, censure, lying and violence. The landholders, lamenting the appearance of these four evils, now resolve to select an individual to establish and maintain order among them, in return for whose efforts they agree to offer appropriate compensation. "Those beings went to the being among them who was the handsomest, the best favoured, the most attractive, the most capable and said to him: come now, good being, be indignant, censure that which should be rightly censured, banish him who deserves to be banished. And we will contribute to thee a proportion of our rice."[5]

According to this narrative, in the original state of nature men lived in idyllic circumstances, in virtual godlike perfection. However, as they began to succumb to their latent passions, they entered a stage of moral decline that culminated in the establishment, by mutual agreement, of the institutions of property and its safeguard. This mutual agreement constituted the basic social contract that established a political society. However, when the political society proved itself incapable of dealing with the security problems that arose as a consequence of a further decline in public morality, it became necessary to establish a state. In so doing, a governmental compact was concluded between the society and one of their number, who was endowed with the political authority originally vested in the society as a result of the initial social contract.[6]

Roman jurists universally rested the power of the emperor and the state upon such an original compact that was presumed to have embodied either the explicit or implicit consent of the people. The medieval and early modern writers also generally adopted this approach to establishing the legitimacy of the state. In the tenth century, Al-Farabi formulated a theory of "renunciation of rights" to account for the origin of the state. He drew an analogy between the situation of man before the creation of the state and the condition of unjust "sale and purchase," that is, a situation where the strong imposes his will on the weak. In such a state of affairs, man, in his business and other social relations, lives in a constant state of fear and threat of conflict. The unsatisfactory nature of this mode of existence eventually drives him to join with others who find themselves in a similar predicament to seek a means of mutual protection. They therefore agree among themselves to renounce part of their inherent rights and autonomy, and to delegate them to a particular individual who will act as the protector of the group, making him their sovereign ruler. This voluntary renunciation of rights, taken in the form of mutual vows and commitments, constitutes a compact between the people and the sovereign that establishes the state.[7]

Similarly, in the eleventh century, Manegold von Lautenbach declared that the state was nothing but the work of man. Kingship, he asserted, was an institution that arose neither naturally nor in consequence of the inherent merit of the person elevated to the throne. The authority vested in the king was given to him by the people as part of the compact that they concluded with him; he was made their ruler so that he should defend them against their oppressors and so that he might establish good order in society by compelling the evil men among them to live in conformity with its mores.[8] However, should the king betray this trust and assume the role of tyrant, Manegold considers him to have broken the compact upon which his authority rests and therefore to be unworthy of further obedience by the people. Manegold compared the tyrant king to a swineherd who was hired to attend to one's pigs, and who was discovered to be butchering them instead of caring for them. In such a case, there would be no question about whether the swineherd should be fired in disgrace, as there should be no question about the appropriate disposition of the tyrannical king. Since the state was based on a contract, a violation of its terms by the king brought about its termination and all obligations on the part of the people similarly came to an end.[9]

In support of these claims concerning the governmental compact as the basis of the state, Maine assures us that the earliest feudal communities were in fact bound together by contract, and that new members were inducted into the community through a contractual procedure. The relation of the feudal lord to his vassals was established by express agreement and anyone who wished to become part of that arrangement did so with a clear understanding of the conditions on the basis of which he was to be admitted. "It is therefore the sphere occupied in them by Contract which principally distinguishes the feudal institutions from the unadulterated usages of primitive races." Although the feudal lord often appeared as a patriarchal chieftain with virtually unlimited powers, his prerogatives were clearly delimited in accordance with customs that could be traced to "the express conditions which had been agreed upon when the infeudation took place."[10]

In the latter part of the medieval period, the theory of the governmental compact became increasingly popular and was argued more forcefully, clearly challenging the naturalist theories. In the fifteenth century, Nicholas of Cusa wrote:

Since by nature all are free, every government—whether it consists in written law or in a living law in the prince . . . is based on agreement alone and the consent of the subjects. For if by nature men are equally powerful and equally free, the valid and ordained authority of one man naturally equal in power with the others cannot be established except by the choice and consent of the others, even as law is also established by consent. Now, since by a general compact human society has agreed to obey its kings, it follows that in a true order of government there should be an election to choose the ruler himself, through which election he is constituted ruler and judge of those who elect him.[11]

By the end of the following century the compact theory had gained broad respectability in Europe. King James of England clearly reflected the idea of a contractual relationship between the monarch and his subjects in a speech delivered to Parliament in 1609. He acknowledged that "the king binds himself, by a double oath, to the observation of the fundamental laws of his kingdom—tacitly, as by being a king, and so bound to protect, as well the people as the laws of his kingdom; and expressly by his oath at his coronation; so as every just king, in a settled kingdom, is bound to observe that paction made to his people, by his laws, in framing his government agreeable thereunto . . . Therefore, all kings that are not tyrants, or perjured, will be glad to bound themselves within the limits of their laws."[12]

In accepting the contractual origin of governments, many theorists reluctantly felt the need to concede that the sovereign power originally rested with the people, since they clearly had to have that which they were supposed to have given away. It also had to be assumed that the people could not conclude the governmental compact with the ruling authority unless it acted in a corporate capacity. That is to say, it could not do so as a mere aggregation of individuals. It was necessary that the people be first organized into a political community capable of concluding a contract that would alienate its inherent sovereignty, either totally or conditionally. On the other hand, it was argued by some that this was an erroneous view, that there was no need to suppose an original coming together of individuals to form a political society, since the existence of such a society is inherent in nature itself. Thus, Bolingbroke argued that "men were directed by nature to form societies, because they cannot by their nature subsist without them, nor in a state of individuality; and since they were directed in like manner to establish governments, because societies cannot be maintained without them, nor subsist in a state of anarchy; the ultimate end of all governments is the good of the people, for whose sake they were made, and without whose consent they could not have been made."[13] Consequently, one need not look beyond the governmental compact to rationalize the corporate behavior of the political community, since the latter evolved naturally and not as a result of the deliberate actions of individuals.[14]

When this later concept fell into disfavor because of its failure to take into consideration the idea of inherent individual rights, it left a conceptual void in the theories designed to account for the manner in which the transition from an aggregation of individuals to a unified political community took place. The postulation by some theorists of a state of nature governed by natural law made it necessary for them to reintroduce the idea of some sort of original contract or agreement to explain how the natural liberty of the individual was legitimately superseded by the rule of a public authority.

One of the first writers in the modern era to deal with the notion of the original social contract in a significant manner was the English clergyman Richard Hooker. Toward the end of the sixteenth century, he attempted to deal with the problem of the relationship of the church to the state by asserting that the former was not necessarily subject to direct divine regulation in all matters. In his view, the institutional laws of the church might be made by men, so long as they were not contrary to the Scriptures. In laying the groundwork for this thesis, Hooker was led to undertake an inquiry concerning the origin of all political authority, which he ultimately found to be rooted in the voluntary consent of the governed.

Hooker began his examination by postulating a state of nature where, in the absence of government and law, without the ability to find a common basis among themselves for the regulation of their conduct to the general advantage, men found themselves in truly desperate straits. This was a general consequence of the fact that the solitary individual is not sufficiently able to satisfy his material needs to the extent necessary for him to lead a life of dignity. "Therefore to supply those defects and imperfections which are in us living single and solely by ourselves, we are naturally induced to seek communion and fellowship with others. This was the cause of men's uniting themselves at the first in politic Societies, which societies could not be without Government, nor Government without a distinct kind of Law." While political society alone may have been sufficient to provide the degree of cooperation needed to complement the deficiencies of the individual in the face of nature, it was not adequate for dealing with the grievances, injuries and wrongs that occurred within the society. It became obvious that it was necessary to establish a regime for the society that could assure the public safety and tranquility; that "there was no way but only by growing unto composition and agreement amongst themselves, by ordaining some kind of government public, and by yielding themselves subject thereunto; that unto whom they granted authority to rule and govern, by them the peace, tranquility, and happy estate of the rest might be procured." They understood that societal instability would remain endemic "except they gave their common consent all to be ordered by some whom they should agree upon: without which consent there were no reason that one man should take upon him to be lord or judge over another."[15] Hooker thus clearly posits a social contract as the predecessor to a later governmental compact.

This argument was adopted in part, at least with respect to the idea of the original social contract, by John Milton, who considered it to be fully self-evident that man was intended by his very nature to be free and autonomous. He wrote: "No man who knows aught can be so stupid to deny that all men naturally were born free, being the image and resemblance of God Himself." Falling back on the doctrine of original sin to explain man's subsequent perversity, Milton suggested that men foresaw that the growing anarchy under which they lived would lead to their ultimate destruction. Wishing to forestall such an eventuality, "they agreed by common league to bind each other from mutual injury, and jointly to defend themselves against any that gave disturbance or opposition to such agreement."[16]

A similar position was staked out on the continent by Juan de Mariana, a Jesuit who deviated in this from the main trends of Catholic thought. According to Mariana, in their original natural state, men lived as nomads, without permanent settlements. They were essentially unrestrained in their conduct, not being under the regime of any law nor under the power of any ruler. The only constraints on their behavior derived from natural instinct and patriarchal tradition. The latter developed, Mariana suggests, because "by an innate impulse the greatest honor in each family was offered to him whom, because of the prerogatives of age, they saw to be superior to the others." As the generations passed and the number of people grew, the numerous family groups formed themselves into tribes, and "a first outline of society seemed to be discernible, though rudimentary and simple." Men, however, were created with many needs and desires that could not be satisfied without entailing great risks to their security. This was done purposively, "to develop their will power and force them to act; so that many a man strove to obviate or meet these disadvantages." Nature was thus a training ground for the development of man's innate capabilities. Ultimately, "as each person relied very greatly on his own powers, men encroached upon the lives and fortunes of the weaker, with no opposition, like the ferocious and solitary wild beast, terrifying some, dreading others." This soon resulted in the growth of associations, not only for defense but for aggression as well. Organized bands began raiding the flocks in the fields and on the farms, seizing whatever they could and violently suppressing any attempt by those assaulted to oppose them. The situation soon became intolerable, with even blood relatives and intimate friends engaging in such violence against each other. Accordingly, "those who were pressed by the more powerful began to draw themselves together with others in a mutual compact of society and to look for someone outstanding in justice and trustworthiness. By his aid they hoped to ward off domestic and foreign injuries, and by establishing justice to restrain and bind down all classes, high, middle and low, by a fair system of law."[17] Thus, Mariana tells us, the state is created by man in consequence of the objective need for cooperative association and for protection, itself the result of man's inherent frailty in the face of brute nature and the violence of his fellows.

One of the first continental European writers to develop more fully the idea of an original social contract as a necessary antecedent to the governmental compact was Johannes Althusius, who wrote at the beginning of the seventeenth century. For Althusius, the political society is composed of numerous associations, both private and public. The "primary association" from which all others derive is the "simple and private association," which he defines as "a society and symbiosis initiated by a special covenant (*pactum*) among the members for the purpose of bringing together and holding in common a particular interest. . . . The efficient causes of this simple and private association and symbiosis are individual men covenanting among themselves to communicate whatever is necessary and useful for organizing and living in private life."[18] Included in this primary category is the "natural association," the family, as well as the primal "civil association," which is a body freely organized by people who "agree among themselves by common consent on a manner of ruling and obeying for the utility both of the whole body and of its individuals."[19] These and larger public associations ultimately constitute the "universal association," which is, according to Althusius, "a polity in the fullest sense, an imperium, realm, commonwealth, and people united in one body by the agreement of many symbiotic associations and particular bodies and brought together under one right."[20] It is the universal association, representing the people, that with the "supreme magistrate enter into a covenant concerning laws and conditions that set forth the form and manner of the imperium and subjection."[21] The social contract, followed later by a governmental compact, thus serves as the key to Althusius's entire system.

The idea that sovereign political power rested originally with the people and was transferred to the rulers by compact, explicit or implicit, was generally accepted by most consent theorists. The issue that remained in contention, however, was the nature and scope of this compact. On the one hand, some writers took the position that the surrender of the autonomous political rights of the people to the ruler was total and irrevocable. On the other hand, it was maintained by their critics that this governmental compact did nothing more than provide for a conditional delegation of power to the rulers. This power was to be used by the latter only for the specific purposes for which it was granted, and was continually subject to recall were it to be abused.

A clear statement of the absolutist position was set forth in ancient times in the writings of the Chinese philosopher Mo Tzu, who was a staunch opponent of Confucius. According to Mo Tzu, in the period before the creation of an organized state, "everyone had his own standard of right and wrong. When there was one man, there was one standard. When there were two men, there were two standards. When there were ten men, there were ten standards. The more people there were, the more there were standards. Every man considered himself as right and others as wrong." Man lived in a situation that would later be called the *state of nature*. "The world was in great disorder and men were like birds and beasts. They understood that all the disorders of the world were due to the fact that there was no political ruler. Therefore, they selected the most virtuous and most able man of the world, and established him as the Son of Heaven."[22]

In other words, according to Mo Tzu, the ruler of the state is chosen by the will of the people in order to rectify the anarchy resulting from the confusion of standards of right and wrong and proper conduct. His primary responsibility is to "unify the standards," since there can be only one standard in the state if order is to be brought out of social chaos. Achieving this goal requires the unqualified subjugation of the people to the ruler. Once established as the absolute authority in the state, the ruler demands that "Upon hearing good or evil, one shall report it to one's superior. What the superior thinks to be right, all shall think to be right. What the superior thinks to be wrong, all shall think to be wrong."[23] It is thus evident that Mo Tzu is advocating that the state must be totalitarian in character, and the authority of the ruler absolute.[24]

In more modern times, arguing that the grant of power under the governmental compact is absolute and irrevocable, Suarez compared the birth of the state to that of a child. The father of the child is indeed responsible for bringing it into existence. However, once born, freedom, reason, and power are granted to the child by God; the father has no right to usurp these. Similarly, the community may or may not choose to bring the state into existence. But, once the state is brought into being, the community can no longer deny it complete freedom from further control. Taking a similar stance, Hugo Grotius sought to refute the arguments of those who deemed it inconceivable that a people might surrender its sovereignty absolutely, without reservation and without power of revocation. He took the position that "any man may legitimately submit himself in private slavery to whomever he pleases. Why then may not an independent people submit itself to one or more persons, completely transferring to them its right to govern itself, and reserving no portion of that right for itself?" Indeed, he suggested, there might be many reasons why a people would elect to surrender completely its right to govern itself and transfer it to an individual or group of people. One such conceivable circumstance might be a fear of destruction by an enemy coupled with the inability to find someone to undertake their defense on any terms other than absolute subjugation. Another comparably dire situation might arise as a result of famine and the fear of starvation, where total surrender of rights to a ruler may be the only viable means of obtaining the critically necessary food.[25]

This argument aroused the special ire of Rousseau, who insisted on the impossibility of founding a "right" of control upon such a basis. Since, in his view, no benefits that could conceivably be forthcoming from a monarch would compensate for the loss of one's liberty, Rousseau dismissed as absurd the idea that a man can rightly alienate his freedom. "Such an act," he insisted, "is null and illegitimate, from the mere fact that he who does it is out of his mind. To say the same of a whole people is to suppose a people of madmen; and madness creates no right." Moreover, he argued that even if a man could alienate himself, he certainly could not alienate his children. Since they were born free men, their liberty belongs to them and is not at the disposal of the parent; only they would have the right to surrender it to another. "It would therefore be necessary, in order to legitimize an arbitrary government, that in every generation the people should be in a position to accept or reject it; but, were this so, the government would be no longer arbitrary."[26]

Other writers maintained that, even if it were possible for a people to alienate its sovereignty, in the absence of an explicit agreement to the contrary there would exist an inherent presumption that such a surrender of power was necessarily conditional. At a minimum, it would entail implicit assurances that the employment of the authority so transferred should be directed to the general welfare of the community. An interesting example of this argument is to be found in a work first published in Japan in the late nineteenth century. In writing of the evolution of government, Nakae Chomin argues that the earliest societies are characteristically devoid of any political system. They are, in effect, in a state of nature, where "the strong control the weak and the clever deceive the stupid. He who intimidates and overpowers others becomes the master and he who fears and submits to others becomes the slave." As a result, chaos prevails and life becomes uncertain. People eventually become weary of wars, conflicts, and general social disorder and yearn for order and peace. At the ripe moment, "a man of talent and virtue appears, fires the hearts of the people, and becomes their sovereign. Having accomplished that, he issues laws to seek immediate peace and order." The people have apparently surrendered their freedom and autonomy to the rule of a sovereign. Why, Nakae asks, did these ancestors willingly submit themselves to the rule of a sovereign, placing their trust and faith in him and accepting the burdens of obligation? The obvious answer is that they could not lead a viable existence as their own masters. However, this does not mean that by accepting the domination of a ruler they thereby alienated their sovereignty for all time. On the contrary, he suggests, "they abandoned their rights for the time being as a temporary expedient, hoping that in later generations, when their descendants' knowledge had gradually increased, they could regain their independence. No such agreement was explicitly made between ruler and subject in the beginning, but when we consider the deeper meaning of monarchy, these are the implications of the relationship between ruler and ruled." However, he concludes, the reason it appears that the transfer of sovereignty was absolute and irrevocable is that "the sovereign who was entrusted with our ancestors' rights as a temporary expedient would not return them to us, and instead insisted that they were his to begin with. Thus, as I have said, the system of absolute monarchy is blindly unaware of its own insolence."[27]

8

The Consent Theory (II)

In Europe, the absolutist position was to receive its most impressive defense in the writings of Thomas Hobbes. He portrayed the state of nature, that is, the "time men live without a common Power to keep them all in awe," to be one in which men are continually at war, or preparing for war, with each other. In such a universe there exist no legal rights either of person or property. "The notions of Right and Wrong, Justice and Injustice have there no place. Where there is no common Power, there is no Law: where no Law, no Injustice."[1] Man's only way out of this chaos is through the use of his reason, which suggests to him the existence of a natural law that can be used as the basis for founding a new political order. The two most fundamental of these natural laws are, first, "That every man, ought to endeavour Peace, as farre as he has hope of obtaining it"; and second, "That a man be willing, when others are so too, as farreforth, as for Peace, and defence of himselfe he shall think it necessary, to lay down this right to all things; and be contented with so much liberty against other men, as he would allow other men against himselfe."[2] Hobbes thus based the state upon a compact between individuals, whereby, for the sake of peace and stability, each of them willingly surrendered the greatest part of his own natural liberty in order that all might escape from the chronic state of war.

These contracting individuals enter into an agreement whereby each transfers his power to some individual or individuals, who henceforth act on behalf of all with the combined power of all. The consequence of such an agreement is the founding of the state. "A Common-wealth is said to be Instituted, when a Multitude of men do Agree, and Covenant, every one, with every one, that to whatsoever Man, or Assembly of Men, shall be given by the major part, the Right to Present the Person of them all, (that is to say, to be their Representative;) every one, as well he that Voted for it, as he that Voted against it, shall Authorise all the Actions and Judgements, of that man, or Assembly of men, in the same manner, as if they were his own, to the end, to live peaceably amongst themselves, and be protected against other men."

The government, in whatever form it is established by the covenant, receives an indefeasible right to direct and set limits to the actions of all members of the society. Not only does the power of the ruler become absolute, but the people forever forfeit all right of dissociation. The contract, once made, is understood by Hobbes to be both irrevocable and indissoluble. He maintains that such absolute government and the virtually total alienation of the people's rights of autonomy derive directly from the very character of the contract, which reflects the consent of the people to its terms. "Because they that have already Instituted a Commonwealth, being therefore bound by Covenant, to own the Actions and Judgements of one, cannot lawfully make a new Covenant, amongst themselves, to be obedient to any other, in any thing whatsoever, without his permission. And therefore, they that are subjects to a Monarch, cannot without his leave cast off Monarchy, and return to the confusion of a disunited Multitude; nor transferre their Person from him that beareth it, to another man, or other Assembly of men."[3]

However, Hobbes places one important limitation on the

absolute authority of the ruler; to legitimately command the unqualified allegiance of his subjects, he must be capable of fulfilling the essential purpose for which the state was brought into being in the first place, namely, that of assuring the security of the people. Where the ruler fails to accomplish this, his subjects become absolved from their obligation of obedience to him. Thus Hobbes writes: "The Obligation of Subjects to the Sovereign is understood to last as long, and no longer, than the power lasteth, by which he is able to protect them. For the right men have by Nature to protect themselves, when none else can protect them, can by no Covenant be relinquished."[4]

From this form of creation of the state, which he calls a "Common-wealth by Institution," Hobbes turns to the question of a state acquired by force, which he refers to as a "Common-wealth by Acquisition." The latter comes into existence "when men singly, or many together by plurality of voyces, for fear of death, or bonds, do authorise all the actions of that Man, or Assembly, that hath their lives and liberty in his Power." In other words, Hobbes asserts the legitimacy of the regime that is imposed on a conquered state by force, even though the conquered people have no alternate practical course of action other than to register their approval of the conquest. Indeed, for Hobbes, there is only a minor distinction between a commonwealth of institution and a commonwealth of acquisition. The former type of state emerges as a consequence of the fear that individuals have of each other, but not of the individual or individuals to whom they agree to transfer their power. In the latter case, the people transfer their power to one whom they also fear. "In both cases they do it for fear: which is to be noted by them, that hold all such Covenants, as proceed from fear of death, or violence, voyd: which if true, no man, in any kind of Common- wealth, could be obliged to Obedience."[5] Here, Hobbes appears to be suggesting that while in the case of the commonwealth by institution the ruler is installed because he is not feared, once in power he is obeyed out of fear just as would be the case in a commonwealth by acquisition. Accordingly, in the final analysis, Hobbes would legitimize *existing* governments on the basis of the force they can bring to bear on any challenge to their authority.

In Hobbes's view, then, the ruler possesses unlimited power, and regardless of how arbitrary or oppressive he may be in the exercise of this power, the people are obligated to render obedience. To resist the supreme authority is to return to a state of anarchy. The rights transferred to him cannot be withdrawn without his consent; for, though not a party to the original social contract, the ruler has subsequently obtained indefeasible rights under it. There is in effect no compact between the people and the ruler they have placed in power. The social contract is only between the prospective citizens of the state, wherein they agree to the necessary establishment of a ruling authority. Sovereignty, which did not exist before the state was established through the covenant, is now brought into being as a necessary consequence of the birth of the state. The person or persons to whom this supreme authority is then assigned come to embody the absolute power of the state.

It seems quite evident that perhaps one of the most serious problems with Hobbes's argument results from his failure to make any clear distinction between the state and its government. He does not distinguish between the sovereign power of the state and those agents or instruments of the state to whom the exercise of this power is entrusted. The establishment of government is an act that is clearly independent of and subsequent to that of the creation of the state. It would therefore be reasonable to assume that the transfer of the sovereign authority of the state to the government must be the result of some further contractual agreement. Otherwise one would have to assume that a group of individuals, who reluctantly alienated their personal rights and autonomy to create an absolutist state that would assure their individual and mutual security, would then simply allow such absolute authority to be arbitrarily and unconditionally turned over to some individual or group of persons. Yet, Hobbes does not deal with this matter, since his sovereign is not a party to the social contract and may therefore act as arbitrarily as he chooses.

Benedict de Spinoza, who also accepted the contractual theory of the origin of political authority, rejected Hobbes's extreme conception of the state of nature as the perennial battleground for a war of all against all, thus necessitating the formation of a civil society. For him, it is sufficient to note that "all men, whether barbarous or civilized, everywhere frame customs, and form some kind of civil state."[6] This occurs because men find the help of others necessary for the satisfaction of even their most elemental needs, and a settled social order offers distinct advantages for the individual. The state, in other words, serves a utilitarian purpose. In this regard, Spinoza writes: "The formation of society serves not only for defensive purposes, but is also very useful, and, indeed, absolutely necessary, as rendering possible the division of labour. If men did not render mutual assistance to each other, no one would have either the skill or the time to provide for his own sustenance and preservation . . . We see that peoples living in uncivilized barbarism lead a wretched and almost animal life, and even they would not be able to acquire their few rude necessaries without assisting one another to a certain extent."[7]

This natural need for society, because of man's inherent inability to discipline his life in accordance with the demands of objective reason, inevitably leads to the need for a state. Spinoza argues that, "if men were so constituted by nature that they desired nothing but what is designated by true reason, society would obviously have no need of laws . . . But human nature is framed in a different fashion: every one, indeed, seeks his own interest, but does not do so in accordance with the dictates of sound reason . . . Therefore, no society can exist without government, and force, and laws to restrain and repress men's desires and immoderate impulses."[8]

The state is thus the conscious and deliberate creation of men, and has been instituted because they recognize that each would gain more than he lost by having settled laws, customs, modes of conduct, and forms of rule made binding upon all. Such a utilitarian conception of the state has been characterized by Lilly as one that regards it "as a fortuitous concourse of men bound by the tie of common advantage; a mere machine, driven by the forces of public and private interest; a sort of huge insurance society, the taxes being the premium."[9]

Nonetheless, the obvious usefulness of the state is such that its very utility would appear to be adequate justification for its existence. Thus, Fred M. Taylor argued:

One need only reflect that the community is an association so extensive as to furnish an authority more nearly free from personal elements than any other association; that the sense of responsibility to a real public opinion makes the reckless more thoughtful, lifts them out of their natural particularity, and enables them to realize in some degree the rationality which alone justifies their possession of authority; and, finally, that the community is an association which brings to the service of justice a physical force so overwhelming that the supremacy of justice is commonly assured without even a resort to that force.[10]

Accordingly, it would seem that while there is nothing in nature to prevent men from taking independent action on their own behalf, the efficacy of doing so through an organized community promises a far greater degree of success.

Given the rational need for the state, Spinoza argues that it must be endowed with the authority and power to carry out its purposes effectively: "For, although men's free judgements are very diverse, each one thinking that he alone knows everything, and although complete unanimity of feeling and speech is out of the question, it is impossible to preserve peace, unless individuals abdicate their right of acting entirely on their own judgement. Therefore, the individual justly cedes the right of free action, though not of free reason and judgement; no one can act against the authorities without danger to the state, though his feelings and judgement may be at variance therewith."[11] The state therefore represents the manifestation of a social compact of a unique kind. It provides the basis for all other societal agreements.

In Spinoza's view, the need for the state is rooted in the very nature of man and it is therefore essential to the viability of civilization. Because of this, the existence of the state cannot depend upon the existence of an explicit verbal or written agreement. The implicit presumption of an agreement is sufficient. Moreover, Spinoza indicates, the state does not necessarily come into existence as the result of the voluntary consent of a group of autonomous individuals. As Hobbes indicated, it may just as well be predicated upon force and conquest. It thus makes no difference, with respect to its validity, whether the state is established by consent or by force. In either case, the sovereign is justified in taking whatever actions he determines to be in the common interest, and the people are fully obligated to obey his commands, regardless of whether they do so through fear or rational judgment. In this regard, Spinoza categorically rejects the notion that a citizen should be permitted to interpret the commonwealth's decrees or laws or determine their acceptability. On the contrary, he argues that every citizen is completely beholden to the state, "all whose commands he is bound to execute, and has no right to decide, what is equitable or iniquitous, just or unjust. . . . the will of the commonwealth must be taken to be the will of all; what the state decides to be just and good must be held to be so decided by every individual."[12]

Spinoza recognized that this abject and total surrender of one's judgment to another appears essentially irrational and would base the authority of the state on an unreasonable and therefore unsound foundation. Since man can never alienate his reason, Spinoza found it necessary to argue that reason itself demands that the individual suspend its operation and subordinate himself unconditionally to the state. "The civil state is naturally ordained to remove general fear, and prevent general sufferings, and therefore pursues above everything the very end, after which everyone, who is led by reason, strives, but in the natural state strives vainly. Wherefore, if a man, who is led by reason, has sometimes to do by the commonwealth's order what he knows to be repugnant to reason, that harm is far compensated by the good, which he derives from the existence of a civil state. For it is reason's own law, to choose the less of two evils;

and accordingly we may conclude, that no one is acting against the dictate of his own reason, so far as he does what by the law of the commonwealth is to be done."[13]

Spinoza insists that the authority of the state must be independent of and superior to any right or power vested in its citizens as private individuals, that is, any rights they may have possessed before they became citizens of the state. As citizens they can have no rights, public or private, other than those granted to them by the state. Accordingly, if any individual or corporate entity, such as an association or a church, succeeds in attaining a position of right or power without the authority of the state, it should be seen as a demonstration of the weakness and inefficiency of the state. If it is to preserve its independence, the state must maintain its supremacy. The state cannot alienate its sovereignty; it cannot legitimately transfer any part of its sovereign rights to any other body or individual.

Nevertheless, in Spinoza's view, the social compact is not absolute in the sense of its being inviolable. Should circumstances affecting the common safety warrant, the compact might be broken. However, the right to make the determination to abrogate the compact rests exclusively with the central authority into whose hands the supreme power has been entrusted. Thus, it is not the people, but the regime alone that has the right to annul the social compact. And, except under such extraordinary circumstances, those who embody the authority and power of the state, its government, are fully obligated to honor the terms of the compact. As a practical matter, reason dictates that the continued existence of a state is dependent to a great degree on its ability to maintain its inner strength, and this is subject to both the fear and the reverence of its subjects. If these are lost or diminished, the state itself becomes vulnerable and is certain to go into decline. Accordingly, the ruling authorities of the state must conduct themselves in such a manner as to retain the respect of the citizens. Should they abuse their power and, acting in contempt of the laws of the state, afflict the citizenry, they will turn "fear into indignation and the civil state into a state of enmity."[14]

Spinoza also draws a distinction between the principles of conduct that may be applied to the state and those that are applicable to individuals. The ancient principle that pacts agreed to must be observed is not an absolute for the state. Each state must give priority to the interests of its own citizens, and cannot reasonably be expected to enter into an agreement with another that would interfere with this objective. Therefore, to observe a treaty that is not found to be in the interest of its own citizens is to act contrary to the very idea and purpose of the state.

When asked to point out the major difference between his views and those of Hobbes, Spinoza replied: "As regards political theories, the difference ... between Hobbes and myself, consists in this, that I always preserve natural right intact, and only allot to the chief magistrates in every state a right over their subjects commensurate with the excess of their power over the power of the subjects. This is what always takes place in the state of nature."[15] In other words, Spinoza maintained that a compact entered into between individuals in a state of nature could not reasonably confer greater legal or moral validity to rules based on it than such rules would have in an entirely nonpolitical state of society. Hobbes, on the other hand, drew a distinction between the relative scopes of natural law, and civil or political law. "The law of nature [which he identifies also with divine laws] doth always and everywhere oblige in the internal court, or that of conscience but not always in the external court, but then only when it may be done with safety."[16] That is, natural law has full sway over man's private moral conduct, but only limited application in his public life. Civil law, on the other hand, according to Hobbes's definition, "is to every Subject, those Rules, the Common-wealth hath Commanded him, by Word, Writing, or other sufficient Sign of the Will, to make use of, for the Distinction of Right, and Wrong; that is to say, of what is contrary, and what is not contrary to the Rule."[17]

Nonetheless, for Hobbes, natural law and civil law are intimately related and intertwined. The laws of nature, which consist of equity, justice, gratitude, and other related moral virtues, he argues, are not really laws in the usual sense of the term; they are instead merely those natural moral imperatives that incline one to seek peace and to render obedience to authority. It is only when the state is actually established that they become operative laws. At that time they become incorporated into the civil law, and are subsequently subject to enforcement by the state. It is then the state that demands that they be obeyed. At the same time, every subject in a state is obligated by covenant to obey the civil law; either the agreement they voluntarily made with each other when the Common-wealth by Institution was established, or the involuntary covenant they were compelled to enter when they were subdued by force and brought into the Common-wealth by Acquisition. In either case, obedience to the civil law was itself a requirement of natural law which forbids breach of a covenant. The law of nature thus commands us to keep all the civil laws. Hobbes thus asserted that civil and natural laws were not intrinsically different kinds of law, but rather different aspects of a common law, of which the written part is called civil law and the unwritten natural law. But, he insisted, "the Right of Nature, that is, the naturall Liberty of man, may by the Civill Law be abridged, and restrained; nay, the end of making Lawes, is no other, but such Restraint; without the which there cannot possibly be any Peace. And Law was brought into the world for nothing else, but to limit the naturall liberty of particular men, in such manner, as they might not hurt, but assist one another, and joyn together against a common Enemy."[18]

John Locke also began his speculations on the origins of the state with the stipulation of certain premises regarding the assumed condition of mankind in a precivic state of nature. By sharp contrast with the position of Hobbes on the matter, Locke considered this state to have been one of perfect freedom and equality and not one of license, "though man in that state have an uncontrollable liberty to dispose of his person or possessions . . . The state of Nature has a law of Nature to govern it, which obliges every one; and reason, which is that law, teaches all mankind who will but consult it, that being all equal and independent, no one ought to harm another in his life, health, liberty, or possessions."[19] Under such conditions, this law of nature provides that each individual is equally endowed with the right to prevent encroachment on his person or property by any other; each man becomes the sole judge and enforcer of the law in his own behalf. However, this presumption of natural equality of right may prove illusory, since nature itself does not endow men equally with the attributes of intelligence and physical strength and prowess. This situation creates certain obvious and serious problems as it skews the equitable operation of the law of nature in practice. The inequities that result from allowing every individual to act as sole guarantor of his own rights generate a demand for the creation of an alternate arrangement. It becomes desirable that a neutral third party, endowed with the capability to enforce its decrees, be empowered to act as the common arbiter of individual rights. Men are thus led to the establishment of a political authority to keep their affairs and mutual relations in proper order. As Locke observes: "I easily grant that civil government is the proper remedy for the inconveniences of the state of Nature, which must certainly be great where men may be judges in their own case, since it is easy to be imagined that he who was so unjust as to do his brother an injury will scarce be so just as to condemn himself for it."[20]

Locke thus conceived the source of the state and all legitimate government to have been in a compact, whereby a number of individuals voluntarily surrendered certain of their rights and powers into the hands of a central external authority. "Wherever, therefore, any number of men so unite into one society as to quit every one his executive power of the law of Nature, and to resign it to the public, there, and there only, is a political or civil society. And this is done wherever any number of men in the State of Nature enter into society to make one People, one body politic under one supreme government; or else when any one joins himself to, and incorporates with, any government already made."[21] However, Locke emphasizes, the social contract does not alienate all the rights that the individual possessed in the state of nature by virtue of the law of nature. The individual transfers to the state only some of his rights and powers in order to enable the state to protect and preserve certain other freedoms and rights, particularly with respect to property. "Though men when they enter into society give up the equality, liberty, and executive power they had in the state of Nature into the hands of the society . . . yet it being only with an intention in every one the better to preserve himself, his liberty and property (for no rational creature can be supposed to change his condition with an intention to be worse), the power of the society or legislative constituted by them can never be supposed to extend further than the common good."[22]

Moreover, and in this Locke also differs fundamentally from Hobbes, those rights not conceded to the society continue to inhere in the individual even after the contract is concluded, and have the same binding force as they did prior to the creation of the state. In other words, the governing authority that is brought into existence through the social contract is in no case absolute; indeed, not only is the state not completely independent of the individual and his residual rights, the extent of its authority is circumscribed by these rights. The power of the ruling authorities is fiduciary, one of trust, which when abused may be revoked by the people who have granted it. "The reason why men enter into society is the preservation of their property; and the end while they choose and authorise a legislative is that there may be laws made, and rules set, as guards and fences to the properties of all the society, to limit the power and moderate the dominion of every part and member of the society." It is unreasonable to suppose that it was the will of the society to grant the government the power to deprive its members of the very protections for which they joined in society and established government in the first place. Therefore, "whenever the legislators endeavour to take away and destroy the property of the people, or to reduce them to slavery under arbitrary power, they put themselves into a state of war with the people, who are thereupon absolved from any farther obedience."[23]

Locke does not draw the distinction between natural

(moral) and civil laws as sharply as Hobbes. Nowhere does he clearly distinguish between those rights and obligations that are created as a consequence of the establishment of the state and its sovereign political authority, and those rights and obligations that are considered to be inherent in man's nature and that are therefore independent of the authority of the state. According to Hobbes, a command by the supreme power in the state is legally valid regardless of whether it might stand up to a test on the grounds of morality or reasonability. For Locke, however, the ultimate validity of such a command is entirely dependent upon whether it appears to be consonant with the natural rights of the people with respect to their persons and their property. In other words, while Hobbes cannot conceive of an instance in which the state could be accused of acting illegally, Locke cannot conceive of a case in which the oppression of the people by the state could ever be legal.

While it could be argued, from an exclusively juridical perspective, that Hobbes is more nearly correct than Locke with respect to the matter of the legal omnipotence of the state, his approach to the question will again be found wanting because of his failure to distinguish between the state and its government. Even according to his own theory, it is the state that constitutes the supreme authority, and not the person or persons entrusted with the powers of the state. Thus, while it may not be possible to place a legal limit on the power of the state, one may argue that it is quite possible to impose substantial legal constraints on the competence and actions of its agents, that is, the government. Locke, on the other hand, apparently failed to take into consideration that a government, legitimately invested with the authority and power of the state, might take actions that are properly deemed to be oppressive of the essential rights of citizens without ever trespassing the bounds of legality. In such a case, it becomes essential to distinguish sharply between civil law and natural law. A right to revolt against the government would have to be justified on the basis of its violation of the citizen's natural rights rather than his legal rights.

To some extent, the ambiguity in Locke's formulation also

reflects a failure to distinguish clearly between the social contract and the governmental compact, which leads to a blurring of the distinction between the state and its government. This problem is evident where Locke writes: "Whensoever, therefore, the legislative shall transgress this fundamental rule of society, and either by ambition, fear, folly, or corruption, endeavour to grasp themselves, or put into the hands of any other, an absolute power over the lives, liberties, and estates of the people, by this breach of trust they forfeit the power the people had put into their hands for quite contrary ends, and it devolves to the people, who have a right to resume their original liberty, and by the establishment of a new legislative (such as they shall think fit), provide for their own safety and security, which is the end for which they are in society."[24] It is obvious that Locke has confused the state with the government here, since he appears to be implying that the governmental forfeiture of power also involves the dissolution of the state, since it is only when the state dissolves that the people can return to their "original liberty," the condition that existed prior to the formation of the political society under the social contract. However, Locke surely does not mean this since the power that he says the people would give to a different set of rulers exists only when they are organized as a political society, that is, as the state. Notwithstanding these weaknesses in his arguments, Locke's refusal to accept the idea of an absolute state has resonated through much of modern democratic political theory, and is considered generally as a significant advance over the consent theory of Hobbes.

In the following century, Rousseau also began his exposition of the origins of the state by positing the intrinsic natural freedom of man in a precivic state of nature. Because man does not live in isolation but in association with others it becomes necessary to order the affairs of men to assure their mutual well-being. "Since no man has a natural authority over his fellow, and force creates no right, we must conclude that conventions form the basis of all legitimate authority among men."[25] As noted in the preceding chapter, Rousseau rejected Grotius's notion that a people can alienate its liberty and make itself subject to an absolute ruler, and would similarly reject the views of Hobbes. Rousseau will not countenance the renunciation of man's essential liberty. The crucial problem of political theory for Rousseau "is to find a form of association which will defend and protect with the whole common force the person and goods of each associate, and in which each, while uniting himself with all, may still obey himself alone, and remain as free as before."[26] The solution that he proposes is an association in which each member surrenders his intrinsic rights to all the others. Where this is done, each member gains from everyone else the same rights he yields to them; the members of such a society lose nothing individually while gaining access to a collective power that is committed to preserving what each possesses. Accordingly, the individuals in a community enter into a social contract that, in effect, demands of each the following fundamental commitment: "Each of us puts his person and all his power in common under the supreme direction of the general will, and, in our corporate capacity, we receive each member as an indivisible part of the whole."[27]

Under this concept, by giving himself unreservedly to the control of all, the individual actually gives himself to no particular person. Each individual in himself thus comes to possess an indivisible and inalienable portion of the collective sovereignty of the whole. In this scheme, there is no governmental compact. The social contract is that which is concluded exclusively between the individuals who thereby constitute themselves as the body politic, the state. Government is merely the instrument of a state that never relinquishes its sovereignty. "Those who hold," says Rousseau, "that the act, by which a people puts itself under a prince, is not a contract, are certainly right. It is simply and solely a commission, an employment, in which the rulers, mere officials of the Sovereign, exercise in their own name the power of which it makes them depositaries. This power it can limit, modify, or recover at pleasure; for the alienation of such a right is incompatible with the nature of the social body, and contrary to the end of the association."[28]

Ultimate legislative or volitional authority must always remain with the people, for while the body politic may delegate its power, it cannot alienate its will. Accordingly, Rousseau argues "that Sovereignty, being nothing less than the exercise of the general will, can never be alienated, and that the Sovereign, who is no less than a collective being, cannot be represented except by himself: the power indeed may be transmitted, but not the will."[29] The people are thus left as intrinsically free after as before the contract. The obligation to render obedience to the government is conditional at best. Only that which is in accord with the general will is deemed to possess the binding force of law, and this general will can only be given direct expression through a popular assembly in which every citizen has a direct vote and the opportunity for articulating his views on any matter under consideration. Rousseau thus rejects the idea of representative government which, from his perspective, would involve the illegitimate transfer of the general will to a handful of citizens. If this were permitted to occur, the people would effectively be reduced to slavery once the elections to such a representative body were concluded, since they would have alienated their shares of the general will. True political sovereignty thus rests only with the totality of the citizens, the body politic, whose sovereign powers are inherently and necessarily unlimited. Thus, "as nature gives each man absolute power over all its members, the social compact gives the body politic absolute power over all its members also; and it is this power which, under the direction of the general will, bears, as I have said, the name of Sovereignty."[30]

Although starting from a radically different perspective, Rousseau winds up at the same point as Hobbes. However, from his standpoint, the political absolutism of the body politic cannot logically be considered as oppressive either of the liberty of the people as a whole or even of individual citizens. In the case of the people, this is self-evident since they are themselves the embodiment of sovereignty—the people as a whole is the state. It is somewhat less obvious with regard to the individual citizen, whose personal will has become subsumed by the general will, which does not necessarily reflect individual desires and preferences.

In Rousseau's concept, the general will is not the same as the aggregate of individual wills. "There is often a great deal of difference between the will of all and the general will; the latter considers only the common interest, while the former takes private interest into account, and is no more than a sum of particular wills: but take away from these same wills the pluses and minuses that cancel one another, and the general will remains as the sum of the differences."[31] The general will, then, can only be determined by extracting from each of the individual wills certain sentiments and inclinations that have relevance for the collectivity. From these, through a complex process of weighing, combining, equating, and balancing, a result is obtained that is substantively different from that which would result from the mere aggregation of individual wills. The general will is thus of a higher order than the will of all. Indeed, in the absence of such a general will, each person, acting in accord with his individual will, would be free to commit himself to a social contract or withdraw from it as he chose. He would have the option of arbitrarily abiding by or refusing to accept the obligations imposed by that fundamental agreement. The same moral force that urged men to enter into the contract in the first place would also demand that they break it when further adherence was perceived to be contrary to their private interests.

Since men, as individuals, are different from one another, with varying needs and desires, it is to be expected that there will not be universal agreement among them on all matters. Each person may thus have an individual will whose expression will be different from or even opposed to the general will that he reflects as a citizen. It is therefore only the original social contract that, by its very nature, requires the unanimous consent of all. "In order then that the social compact may not be an empty formula, it tacitly includes the undertaking, which alone can give force to the rest, that

whoever refuses to obey the general will shall be compelled
to do so by the whole body. This means nothing less than
that he will be forced to be free."[32]

Therefore, according to Rousseau, once the social contract
is concluded and the state is established, unanimity is no
longer required and, indeed, would be impracticable given
the diversity among men. Henceforth, a majority vote of the
parties to the social contract is considered sufficient to determine the general will. Recognizing the obvious contradiction between the idea of majority rule, which subjugates
the will of the minority, and the principle of each individual's
intrinsic freedom and autonomy, Rousseau proposed the following highly contentious rationalization: By entering into
the social contract, "the citizen gives his consent to all the
laws, including those which are passed in spite of his opposition, and even those which punish him when he dares
to break any of them." In a political society every human
being may be regarded both as a morally autonomous individual and as a citizen. In his role as citizen, the individual
can never be considered apart from the society as a whole;
he is an integral and inseparable part of the body politic, his
will contributing to the formation of the sovereign general
will to which he must be subservient. In other words, he is
a constituent element of the very authority that coerces him.
Rousseau argues that the general will reflects the essence of
the wills of all the members of the state, by virtue of which
they have obtained civil freedom and citizenship. Accordingly, when a law is proposed in the popular assembly and
the people are asked to vote, this vote does not constitute
a referendum by which the people will accept or reject the
matter under consideration. What they are being asked to
vote on is whether or not they think the proposed legislation
is in conformity with the general will, which is essentially
their true will. "Each man, in giving his vote, states his
opinion on that point; and the general will is found by counting votes. When, therefore, the opinion that is contrary to
my own prevails, this proves neither more nor less than that
I was mistaken, and that what I thought to be the general
will was not so. If my particular opinion had carried the day

I should have achieved the opposite of what was my will: and it is in that case that I should not have been free."[33]

Rousseau's argument here may be seen to be substantially the same as that of Hobbes; namely, that by virtue of the consent freely given to the original social contract, all subsequent acts of the state that was established by that contract become the acts of the contracting party, like it or not. Since such acts are therefore the true expressions of the individual's will, even though he mistakenly has opposed them, he nonetheless is absolutely bound to accept their legitimacy and conduct himself accordingly—he has no recourse but to obey. With Rousseau the doctrine of popular sovereignty receives perhaps its most extreme formulation.

Although Rousseau clearly distinguishes between the state and its government, he fails to draw a coherent distinction between the autonomous authority of the state as an institution and the power of the people as a political community. While he characterizes government as a mere instrument for executing the will of the state, he makes this will practically identical with popular sentiment. The theoretical impact of this on the authority and stability of government is devastating. Whereas Locke limited the power of the government, Rousseau virtually annihilates it. In his view, the government does not embody the will of the state. At most, its duties are strictly limited to administrative acts. "What then is government? An intermediate body set up between subjects and the Sovereign, to secure their mutual correspondence, charged with the execution of the laws and the maintenance of liberty, both civil and political."[34] But even this limited power is constantly subject to revocation. "The moment that the people legitimately assembled as a sovereign body, the jurisdiction of the government wholly lapses, the executive power is suspended, and the person of the meanest citizen is as sacred and inviolable as that of the first magistrate; for in the presence of the person represented, representatives no longer exist."[35] Locke also maintained that it is the people who should have the ultimate power to determine who should rule on their behalf. However, he would accord an inherent legal validity to any act of the government other than those that were so clearly and oppressively in violation of the rights of the individual such as to justify revolution. For Rousseau, on the other hand, the government simply has no legislative powers. To be valid, all laws must be enacted directly by the people. Thus, while Locke considered ultimate sovereign power to be held in reserve by the people, it was only to be exercised in extreme cases. For Rousseau, however, since there is a complete identity between sovereignty and the general will, the sovereign power was to be exercised by the people on a continuing basis.

It has been shown that for Hobbes, Spinoza, Locke, and Rousseau, the social contract, the constitutive agreement between the members of the community, represents the only valid founding pact. Most subsequent writers on consent theory, however, maintained that both the social contract and the governmental compact were essential to account for the state and its political authority. Samuel Pufendorf thus criticized Hobbes's contractual scheme as conferring both too much and too little power upon the sovereign to be a serviceable concept of the genesis of the state. Pufendorf took exception to Hobbes's notion of a single pact that simultaneously establishes a state and institutes an absolute sovereign, before whom the individual rights of the parties to the social contract are completely subjugated. He considered that Hobbes failed to recognize the necessity of a process that would first bring separate individuals into association through a pact, thereby creating a group that would be intrinsically capable of negotiating a mutually binding contract with the sovereign. Pufendorf also objected to Hobbes's conception because, in the absence of a governmental compact, the disobedience of a single person who was party to the social contract could be construed as effectively nullifying that agreement, thereby justifying anarchy.[36] Indeed, Pufendorf not only insisted on the need for both contracts, he also suggested that a constitutional decree was required as an indispensable instrument for the foundation of the state.

Anticipating Rousseau, Pufendorf also saw the idea of a "general will" as an essential concept in the genesis of the state. He argued that the difficulties in determining what best served the common interests of the people "may be cured by uniting the wills of all in a perpetual bond, or by so constituting affairs that there will be for the future but one will for all in those matters which serve the end of society." But the only way in which this unification of wills can take place would be for every individual to subordinate his will to one person or a council "so that whatever that man or council shall decree on matters necessary to the common security, must be regarded as the will of each and every person. For whoever voluntarily grants his power to another is held to agree with his will. . . . When such a union of wills and strength has been made, then there finally arises a state, the most powerful of moral societies and persons."

This contract is founded on the basis of individual rights, and is entered into voluntarily for the express purpose of individual self-preservation. Accordingly, the individual retains the right to emigrate as well as the possibility of only conditional adherence to the contract; that is, if the individual does not agree with the community's decision regarding the form of government it wishes to accept, he may elect to secede from the political association.[37] Accordingly, before the state becomes a reality, there must be a decree enacted by a majority of the original adherents to the social contract that stipulates the form of government that the state is to have. Once this is proclaimed, it becomes binding on all except those who made their original acceptance of the contract conditional. "For until they have settled this point, nothing that makes for the common safety can be steadily carried out." The final stage in the formation of the state is the negotiation and conclusion of the governmental compact whereby the ruler or rulers bind themselves to "care for the common safety and security," of the community, in return for its obedience. This union of wills transforms the state into "one person."[38]

9

Critique of the Consent Theory

The variations on the theme of the state emerging as the direct consequence of a social contract into which men are bound to enter all share certain fundamental assumptions. The consent theories all begin with the premise of the existence of an original nonpolitical community that consists simply of an aggregate of independent individuals. This primeval condition is usually characterized as the state of nature, in which there exist no rules to regulate human conduct other than the laws of nature. According to Locke, reason dictates that since all men are equal and independent, no one ought to harm another in his life, health, liberty, or possessions. The normal condition in the state of nature is therefore presumed to be one of peace. The idyll is disrupted when conflicts eventually do arise as a consequence of the simultaneous pursuit of their individual natural rights by two or more members of the community. But, since each individual is autonomous and therefore the sole judge and defender of his natural rights, there are no reliable and consistently peaceful means of resolving disputes available to the community as a whole. The uncertainties that result from such a situation serve to disturb the general tranquility, and generate a desire to establish some sort of communal authority that will act as the judge of all and the executive agent of the society in the regulation of its affairs. Rousseau's conception of the state of nature is quite similar to that of Locke, except that he speaks of it as an ideal, rather than as the actual primitive historical condition of mankind.

Hobbes, far more concerned with demonstrating the necessity and legitimacy of absolute political authority than in establishing a theoretical basis for individual rights, placed greater emphasis on negative aspects of human personality, and thus characterized the nonpolitical natural condition of man as one of extreme anarchy. In his view, man's most fundamental interests are inherently antagonistic to those of his neighbor; so much so, in fact, that they give rise to a state of constant war of each man against his fellow. This should not be surprising, because the primary natural right with which each human is endowed is the liberty to use his natural strengths and capacities to protect and preserve himself, and generally to advance his own interests. However, reason soon makes it evident that complete reliance on one's self in the struggle for self-preservation may prove counterproductive in the long run. One can never be certain that another will not prove stronger and better able to prevail. At the same time, reason also informs him that his purposes can be achieved with greater certainty and efficacy in the long run if he would consent to join with the other members of the community in an agreement whereby they would fuse their individual powers into a common superior power that would have the strength to compel obedience by all of the members of the community to a regime that established and maintained peace. Men thus enter into a social contract in order to better assure the preservation of their lives and general well-being, an act that is perfectly consistent with each individual's natural right to take whatever steps he deems necessary for his self-preservation.

Hobbes, reflecting his concern with establishing an unimpeachable ground for sovereign political authority, sought to make a convincing case for the absolute character of the state by basing it directly on the social contract. By contrast, the theories of Locke and Rousseau, pursued to their logical conclusions, would prove subversive of any central political authority. This is fully apparent in the conception of Rousseau which fundamentally rejects the very notion of state authority, and makes the validity of all legislative acts entirely dependent upon absolute popular consent. Locke's approach would also undermine the authority of the state because it includes a right on the part of the people to resist the enforcement of law in certain cases. Since the determination of which instances justify political disobedience is made by the people, there can be no case in which they may not assert this right. Consequently, the validity of all laws becomes entirely contingent upon their acceptance as proper and expedient by the very people whose actions they are intended to regulate. Thus, although the theories of Locke and Rousseau differ significantly, the end result would be roughly the same.

It is evident that all the contract theories are predicated on the existence of a natural law that is taken to refer to the imperatives governing the instinctive conduct of living beings, both man and animal. The most fundamental principle of natural law, and the one upon which all its other tenets are based, is that of the natural drive of all living beings for self-preservation, as well as to satisfy those desires that derive from man's inherent nature. The laws of nature are thus not commands to do or refrain from doing particular acts. They contain, as Thomas H. Huxley put it, "nothing but a statement of that which a given being tends to do under the circumstances of its existence, and which, in the case of a living being, it is necessitated to do if it is to escape certain kinds of disability, pain, and ultimate dissolution."[1]

In discussing those "natural laws wherewith we conceive every individual to be conditioned by nature, so as to live and act in a given way," Spinoza calls attention to certain of their essential characteristics that may logically engender extreme consequences. Using the simile of fish, who are naturally conditioned to devour those smaller than themselves, he suggests that "the greater devour the less by sovereign natural right. For it is certain that nature taken in the abstract has sovereign right to do anything she can; in other words, her right is coextensive with her powers." However, since the power of nature is only the aggregate of the separate powers of its individual elements and components, "it follows that every individual has sovereign right to do all that he can; in other words, the rights of an individual extend to the utmost limits of his power as it has been conditioned. Now it is the sovereign law and right of nature that each individual should endeavor to preserve itself as, without regard to anything but itself; therefore this sovereign law and right belongs to every individual, namely, to exist and act to its natural conditions." Spinoza sees no grounds for distinguishing between man and the other components of nature with respect to the operation of the laws of nature. Similarly, there are no natural grounds for drawing distinctions between those possessing sound reason and others, such as fools and madmen. "Whatsoever an individual does by the laws of nature it has a sovereign right to do, inasmuch as it acts as it was conditioned by nature, and cannot act otherwise."[2]

Pursuing this thought, Huxley goes on to observe that it is the natural right of the tiger to seek its prey regardless of whether it is animal or human. But, if we should deny that tigers have the right to torment and devour man, we are really impeaching, not the behavior of tigers, but the order of nature. Accordingly, he suggests that the natural right that one might deduce from such a law of nature is simply a way of stating the fact that there is, in the nature of things, no reason why a man having any particular tendencies to action should not feel free to carry them out. Huxley writes:

The ceaseless and pitiless "struggle for existence" which obtains throughout the whole world of living beings is, in truth, the inevitable consequence of the circumstance that each living being strives knowingly, or ignorantly, to exert all its powers for the satisfaction of its needs; and asserts a tacit claim to possess (to the exclusion of all other beings) all the space on the earth's surface which it can occupy and to appropriate all the subsistence which it can utilize. The state of sentient nature, at any given time, is the resultant of the momentarily balanced oppositions of millions upon millions of individuals, each doing its best to get all it can and to keep what it gets; each, in short, zealously obeying the law of nature and fighting tooth and nail for its natural rights. This is the *ne plus ultra* of individualism; and whenever individualism has unchecked sway, a polity can no more exist than it can among the tigers who inhabit the jungle. It is, in fact, the sum of all possible anti-social and anarchistic tendencies.[3]

Another meaning ascribed to the laws of nature is that of hypothetical commands that guide volitional human conduct. These are presumed to derive either from divine intervention or nature itself. Since they are not the product of human invention, these laws are conceived of as having absolute and universal validity. They are held to be binding for all peoples, everywhere and at all times. The theory of natural law, which has played such a prominent role in the history of political and juridical thought, with its ideas of the "natural," "inalienable," or "imprescriptible" rights of man, generally makes use of the term in this sense. Although there is no compelling reason to link belief in the existence of such a natural law to acceptance of the notion that there once existed a state of nature that was governed by this law, such a linkage has been made by most natural-law writers.

The conceptual bases for the contract theory of the state may be criticized on a number of grounds. First of all, the very notion that there is a distinction between the natural condition of primitive man and the presumably nonnatural state of man in political society is highly problematic. It could as easily be argued that since man is himself a part of nature, all of his actions, at any stage of his development throughout history, are intrinsically natural. Indeed, to state that something *exists* is equivalent to stating that it is *natural*. Thus, the use of the term natural by the contract theorists tends to create distinct categories of being that are by no means self-evident.

Second, the idea of natural law providing an absolute guide to human conduct is also very troublesome. Though one may conceive of an absolute natural law, its actual prescriptions for man must necessarily be relative, since the receipt, un-

derstanding, and application of its stipulations must be me-
diated through each individual's reason, which is hardly uniform in quality among the great diversity of people. What
the outcomes of such a process will be will depend greatly
upon objective and contingent factors that emerge from the
varying circumstances of social, economic, and political life.
These will influence the way a particular individual thinks,
and therefore how he will respond to various situations and
needs. As a practical matter, the notion of an absolute natural law thus becomes transformed into one that may be
subject to more than one legitimate interpretation.

A third difficulty entails the question of the efficacy of
natural law in determining actual as opposed to ideal conduct. Whether natural laws are considered to be the commands either of the deity or of nature, there are no apparent
natural means by which compliance can be enforced. Such
laws are able to affect actual human behavior only to the
extent that they can impose themselves on the consciences
of men. In essence, then, natural laws are nothing other than
moral laws. Such laws may indicate how men ought to conduct themselves, but they cannot dictate what men must do.
It is only when and if these natural laws are adopted by the
dominating political power, and are transformed into positive or civil laws, that they can be enforced. It is thus the
idealistic character of natural law, rather than its applicability
in practice, that has made it attractive as the object of appeal
by those desirous of bringing about a change from what exists
to what ought to be. As a result, natural law has long served
as a basis for argument in favor of social and political reform.
The fact that the principles of natural law are held to originate in human reason, in the individual conscience, rather
than in the commands of established political authorities,
has given it a far-reaching influence, particularly as traditional institutions and other sources of law lose their sanctity
and credibility, or outlive their utility. Natural law thus remains a set of ideal principles rather than an operative system
of law for the ordering of political society.

A fourth issue with respect to natural law, even when its
meaning is restricted to the moral ideals that should govern

human conduct, is whether it is reasonable to assume that it ever had the moral authority that would have allowed it to effectively regulate human conduct even in a completely nonpolitical state of nature, as is generally argued or implied by social contract theorists. The difficulty becomes apparent when one attempts to imagine the conditions that may actually have prevailed in a precivil state of nature. Without the imposition of rules of conduct by means of the authority structure of the state, the only natural law principles that might reasonably be assumed to have any effect on human behavior would be those that related to the natural instincts of all living beings to promote their individual self-preservation. Under the regime of such egocentric principles, it is to be expected that passions and momentary inclinations rather than reason would govern men's actions, and, as Hobbes suggests, an unrelenting and pitiless struggle for perseverance would ensue. Under such conditions, it hardly seems reasonable to assume that individuals would calmly arrive at the conclusion that every other individual had similar natural rights, and that those rights merited respect by all, regardless of whether the other individuals were capable of ensuring their rights through their own efforts. Indeed, as observed by Thomas H. Green, the very postulation of such a theory requires that it be formulated in terms that cannot have any meaning except with regard to societies that are already regulated by law or custom, that is, civil societies. "Natural right," as right in a state of nature which is not a state of society, is a contradiction. There can be no right without a consciousness of common interest on the part of members of a society. Without this there might be certain powers on the part of individuals, but no recognition of these powers by others as powers of which they should allow the exercise, nor any claim to such recognition; and without this recognition or claim to recognition there can be no right."[4]

Moreover, in the absence of rights as such in a state of nature, even the notion of "morality" becomes overly ambiguous. In a social and public context, morality is usually conceived in terms of the acknowledgment of and respect for the rights of others. In a prepolitical state of nature, however, it seems most unlikely that the concept of a moral obligation to observe agreements concluded among individuals would ever arise, or have any great significance if it did.

The essential difficulty with the whole concept seems to be the misleading manner in which the basic problem of the state has been formulated by the contract theorists. Proceeding from the assumption that all individuals in a state of nature are endowed with a natural personal right to freedom of action, the question is asked: How can we justify the usurpation of that right by the state, and its assertion of authority to constrain man's conduct? But, as already suggested, the fundamental premise of this whole approach is questionable. No sufficient basis has been laid for the assumption that the individual is endowed with a natural right to freedom. One could as easily argue that nature only grants the individual powers, not rights, and power does not necessarily confer right.

It would therefore seem equally reasonable to suggest that, in any hypothetical prepolitical state of nature, the aggression and oppression that one would be likely to suffer at the hands of others would probably far exceed that to which he would be subjected by even the most tyrannical government. From this perspective, the creation of a common political authority would represent a significant improvement in the state of an individual's personal security and general well-being by subjecting him, as well as all others, to a known and clearly defined paramount force, rather than to the uncertainty and caprice of random individual forces. Under such circumstances, the subordination of the individual to the authority of the state becomes absolutely necessary; if he does not submit voluntarily, then he must be brought to do so by compulsion. In earlier times, it was a common argument that the individual could always leave the jurisdiction of his state for another, if he was dissatisfied with the way it functioned. Thus, the fact of an individual continuing to remain in a state was taken as implying tacit consent to its authority over him. However, as Hume pointed out in response to those who argue such a position, this presumed right of emigration has little real meaning for many if not most people. "Can we seriously say that a poor peasant or artisan has a free choice to leave his country when he knows no foreign language or manners and lives from day to day by the small wages he acquires? We may as well assert that a man by remaining in a vessel, freely consents to the dominion of the master, although he was carried on board while asleep and must leap into the ocean and perish the moment he leaves her."[5]

From the perspective of the individual, the power of the state over the lives of its citizens is clearly its greatest and most awesome attribute. If one has no ultimate control over his own life, all other rights secured for him by the state are greatly diminished in value. The very ability of the state to exercise such a power over the individual's life surely refutes the notion that the existence of the state can be morally justified on the basis of individual consent, whether the latter is presumed to be tacit or explicit. It seems quite unreasonable to suggest that an individual, in order to secure certain other rights, would willingly surrender to another control of the most fundamental right of all, the right to life, without which all other rights are rather meaningless. Even an absolutist like Hobbes, who insisted that the individual was completely subordinate to the state, nonetheless held the right of self-preservation to be inalienable, and made it an exception to the general principle of state supremacy. Rousseau, on the other hand, in his determination to defend the right of the sovereign power to condemn the criminal to death, is forced to resort to the rather specious assertion that "it is in order that we may not fall victims to an assassin that we consent to die if we ourselves turn assassins."[6]

The necessity for such dubious justifications for the state's ultimate control over the life of the individual vanishes when political authority is presumed to be founded not on the will of the individual but on that of the people acting as a corporate body. Thus, for example, the right of the state to punish the criminal, even to the extent of taking his life, is grounded in the same authority that governs the rest of its activities. Lawlessness is made punishable by the state not because it constitutes a breach of the contract between the individual and the community but for the sake of maintaining order in the state. Consequently, the punitive measures adopted by the state are generally intended and designed, for the most part, to be reformatory and preventive rather than merely retributive.

The social life of man as we have known it throughout history, conditioned to a large degree by the scarcity of those things that men consider valuable and worthy of possession, reflects a relentless struggle to reconcile the individual's respective needs and desires with the competing interests of others. Under such circumstances, the notion that everyone is endowed with a natural liberty to do as he pleases seems quite unfounded and unrealistic. The only real question is whether the conflicts between competing individual interests are to be settled directly by those immediately involved or concerned, in accordance with the relative strengths of their natural endowments of power, or by a third and presumably neutral party, a disinterested arbiter. The latter would have to be a common central authority capable of compensating for the disparate strengths of the contenders, thereby transforming the conflict into one between equals and providing the basis for an equitable resolution of the matter at issue.

To the extent that we can ascribe any freedom to the individual, other than the moral idea of freedom of the will or conscience, it can only refer to a particular sphere of activity wherein the individual may claim the right to do as he pleases, undisturbed by others. However, such a right can hardly exist in a prepolitical state of nature where the more powerful individual may impose his will on one weaker than himself with impunity. Such a right can only exist and be guaranteed in a civil state. And civil freedom, by contrast with hypothetical natural liberty, is double-edged, having both positive and negative aspects. A grant of civil freedom is positive insofar as it permits one to perform certain acts unhindered by others. It is negative in that it simultaneously imposes a restriction on the individual, denying him the right to interfere with the identical positive freedoms of others. It seems evident that a social contract, as conceived by the consent theorists, could have no legal force; contractual rights cannot exist where there is no already existing political authority capable of promulgating and enforcing the civil laws by which such rights might be assured. Since the social contract as such could only be considered an expression of popular sentiment but would not necessarily be binding, having been concluded outside the framework of enforceable law, it could not realistically serve as a basis for any subsequent claims of legal rights and obligations.

Proponents of the contract theory who are sensitive to this problem therefore tend to place their emphasis not so much on the legality of the hypothetical social contract as on its assumed moral force. Hence their concern with justifying the existence of the state on moral grounds. However, critics of the contract theory argue that the demand for a moral justification of the state is unnecessary. As long as it does not render the individual any less free than he would be without it, the authority of the state does not require moral justification. They argue that there is no presumption of unwarranted interference with individual autonomy that requires rationalization.

The underlying reason that the search for a moral basis for the state has been so persistent appears to be, at least partly, a result of the confusion that has existed between the idea of the state and that of government, between the repository of sovereign political authority and the particular agents in whose hands its exercise happens to be vested at a particular time. It is quite understandable that the abhorrence of anarchy would evoke a felt need to conjure up a rationale to explain why even an oppressive or irresponsible monarch or oligarchy should not be overthrown. But there is no sound reason for framing the argument in terms of a justification for the very existence of the state and sovereign political authority.

It could be argued that, to the extent the state requires justification, this is provided empirically by the essential role the state plays in the organization and development of human society. Willoughby writes: "The existence of the State is *rationally* justified because the result of the exercise of its authority is in all cases, as a matter of fact, to preserve freedom rather than to destroy it, to enforce rights rather than to crush them, to check certain acts in order that more important and more numerous acts may be made freely possible."[7] The same point has been made most recently by Paul Weiss, who argues that a central concern of politics is to make the best possible use of whatever means may contribute to enabling people to live together in harmony, while generally benefitting them individually to a greater extent than would otherwise be the case. The state is clearly such a means. "Questions of rights and duties, of obedience and service for it refer to what must be acknowledged and supported in order that such outcomes be efficiently and effectively achieved. Although there could come a time when the functions of a state and its government were encompassed within a larger enterprise, there never will be a time when the state and government are rightly eliminated, since there are precious goods which they alone enable one to obtain. Without these, large numbers of people will not live together equitably for more than short periods."[8]

With regard to the question of the moral basis of the state, the issue of morality may be seen to be relevant only with respect to the extent and manner in which the authority and power of the state are exercised; that is, whether the government acts in accordance with accepted moral standards or guidelines. The moral parameters of any given society, that determine the manner in which human conduct is regulated to comport with the prevailing general sense of moral right and justice, may derive from one or more sources. They may be based on the speculations of unfettered reason, on the presumably eternal and immutable principles of right and wrong set forth by a divine author, on the dictates of the autonomous conscience of man, or on the basis of utilitarian principles recommended by experience. Which one or combination of these will predominate in a particular situation will depend on the stage of cultural development of the people concerned, the character of their religious and traditional beliefs, and other social and economic factors.

In principle, then, the laws or rules of conduct promulgated by the government of a given state may be considered as vindicated morally to the extent that they conform with the accepted standards of public morality within the society. As a practical matter, however, the problem of assessing the moral standing of governments is far more complex than this would suggest. The state cannot simply concern itself with assuring that its regime conducts itself in consonance with a postulated moral ideal. Given the natural differences among people, even within a relatively homogeneous society, and the range of social, economic and political contingencies that may emerge both from within and externally to the state that may affect the well-being of the society, the state may be required to institute a regulatory regime that bears a less than completely desirable correspondence to the moral ideal. Moreover, it may be especially difficult to assess the relative moral merit of alternate policy choices. In other words, the state must cope with realities in a manner that may not always square with the moral ideals of its society. Finally, it may prove undesirable to employ the power of the state on a continuing basis to enforce patterns of societal conduct in spheres of action that might better be pursued voluntarily through broad acceptance of moral imperatives. This could result in the devaluation of public morality to mere obedience to the state out of fear of coercion, without reference to the compelling validity of moral principles. Where obedience is based predominantly on the threat of coercion, it is likely to lapse as the threat diminishes.

Although it is clear that most contract theorists do not ground their conceptions on the supposition that the social contract actually took place, but rather on the proposition that it is conceivable that such an event occurred, this latter proposition is quite dubious at best. The social contract theory of the origin of political authority simply cannot be substantiated from a historical perspective. For one thing, there are no historical records dating to those primeval periods when such compacts are assumed to have been concluded; for another, the study of contemporary "primitive" societies suggests the extreme improbability of such a contract, verbal or otherwise, ever having been concluded. The theory presupposes that the parties to the contract are individuals, while the historical evidence tends to show that in early times it was the family, and not the individual, that was the primary social unit. In fact, it would appear that in the primitive world the individual as such counted for very little, either from the standpoint of the law or from the perspective of the political authorities. As Maine concludes, in his examination of primitive law: "The movement of progressive societies has been uniform in one respect. Through all its course it has been distinguished by the gradual dissolution of family dependency and the growth of individual obligation in its place. The Individual has been steadily substituted for the Family as the unit of which civil laws take account."[9] Indeed, the very notion of individuals having either the right or the power to make such a binding covenant would seem to be quite alien to primitive modes of thought. Anthropological research also suggests that the further back we go in the history of civilization, the more common it is for property to be communally rather than privately held. This clearly contradicts the supposition of contract theory that men voluntarily subordinate their individual property and other rights to the state in return for security and tranquility. Moreover, if this characterization of society at the dawn of recorded history is generally true, it seems quite improbable that in an even earlier period, when the social contract is imagined to have been negotiated and agreed to, an aggregate of individuals could have carried out such a sophisticated enterprise, even if we accept the notion that people at such a primitive stage of cultural development would ever have conceived of the idea of a contract in the first place.

As a practical matter, serious questions must be raised about even the theoretical feasibility of obtaining the unanimous consent of a large number of individuals to alienate their natural rights and private property at a given moment, in modern no less than in primeval times. Without such unanimity the rights of the nonconsenting individual would have to be taken from him by compulsion, negating the essence of the social contract and its consequent principle of political obligation. This point was argued explicitly by Edmund Burke: "If men dissolve their ancient incorporation in order to regenerate their community, in that state of things each man has a right, if he pleases, to remain an individual. Any number of individuals, who can agree upon it, have an undoubted right to form themselves into a state apart and wholly independent. If any of these is forced into the fellowship of another, this is conquest and not compact. On every principle which supposes society to be in virtue of a free covenant, this compulsive incorporation must be null and void."[10] This issue was also raised earlier, in the seventeenth century, by Robert Filmer, who wrote in his *Observations Concerning the Originall of Government*: "Certainly it was a rare felicity, that all men in the world at one instant of time should agree together in one mind to change the natural community of all things into private dominion: for without such a unanimous consent it was not possible for community to be altered: for if but one man in the world had dissented, the alteration had been unjust, because that man by the law of nature had a right to the common use of all things in the world; so that to have given a propriety of any one thing to any other, had been to have robbed him of his right to the common use of all things."[11]

Filmer also called attention to the extreme physical difficulties that would be encountered in an attempt to obtain the necessary unanimous consent to the social contract; impediments so great as to make the idea impracticable. In his tract *The Anarchy of a Limited or Mixed Monarchy*, Filmer argued that it would take nothing short of a miracle to spontaneously bring a great many people together in a single place at a precise moment in time to conclude the agreement. It would have to be spontaneous, in his view, because otherwise there would have to be someone who was authorized to stipulate the time and place for such a gathering, and this would require the prior existence of the political society that is to be established by the social contract. "For except by some secret miraculous instinct they should all meet at one time, and place, what one man, or company of men less than the whole people hath power to appoint either time or place of elections, where all be alike free by nature? and without a lawful summons, it is most unjust to bind those that be absent. The whole people cannot summon itself; one man is sick, another is lame, a third is aged, and a fourth is under age of discretion: all these at some time or other, or at some place or other, might be able to meet, if they might choose their own time and place, as men naturally free should."[12]

Finally, as has already been made clear, for a social contract to be considered valid, it would have to be based on the full acknowledgment by the parties participating in the agreement of the mutual rights and obligations to one another that such a contract would entail. But if we postulate the existence of such a general awareness of the concepts of mutual rights and obligations in a community, it would seem that there also exist those sentiments of mutual and collective interests that underlay the formation of the state. And if this is the case, then what is the particular significance of the contract, since it merely serves as a formal endorsement of the political sentiment that already exists—it does not create anything new. As Green asks: "Given a society of men capable of such consciousness of obligation . . . in what does it differ from a political society?"[13]

10

Conclusion

What, then, is the origin of the state? Is it a social phenomenon natural to man, or is it an artificial construct conceived by him? We have reviewed the divine, patriarchal, organic, force, and consent theories of the genesis of the state and political authority, and have found them all inadequate in one respect or another. Yet, there are elements in them that seem worthy of further consideration. Each speaks to us from a different perception of the universe and man's place in it.

Even a cursory review of the history of the twentieth century will reveal a number of examples of states being created out of whole cloth, almost always by force, and usually either as a by-product of war or an existing power vacuum. Some states emerged in the wake of the withdrawal of colonial powers from their overseas possessions, often becoming established as such within territories frequently delimited by those powers solely for their own administrative convenience, without regard to the nature of the populations encompassed thereby. Others were arbitrarily established to serve the purposes of external powers, while still others were disestablished for the same reasons. Thus, from a strictly historical standpoint, the evidence seems to favor the force theory of the state. Even though it may not be able to establish conclusively that all states, especially the earliest, were founded in this way, it can hardly be disputed with regard to our own time. However, despite the fact that a state, or even all states, may be established by force in one form or another, the force theory fails to establish the legitimacy of state authority, unless one accepts the proposition that "might makes right," and it is the legitimacy of state power that is being challenged today in numerous parts of the globe. Thus, although the force theory may explain the rise of the state and political authority, it is not an adequate explanation of why it is accepted in some cases and rejected in others.

The naturalist theories seem to offer some insights, which, in conjunction with the force theory, may be able to account for this inconsistency. In some instances, it might conceivably be believed that a particular state is endowed with divine authority once it is established and that acceptance of its authority is incumbent upon the faithful. Of course this explanation would be of little relevance to a secular society, or one with an incompatible religious tradition. In the latter cases, particularly in highly traditional societies, the patriarchal theory may well explain the acceptance of the state's authority as the simple extension of that of the traditional clan or tribal chiefs. However, the patriarchal theory is not likely to make much impression in contemporary times in more culturally sophisticated societies. In the latter, we would be tempted to turn once again to consent theory, even though it seems quite improbable that more than a few states ever came into being through the processes it describes. But consent theory does have the advantage of its appeal to reason, and therefore continues to play a major role, in one form or another, in contemporary political thought.

With regard to consent theory, in essence we have put aside the idea of an original social contract because of the difficulty of conceiving of the state as an outcome of the spontaneous decisions of an aggregate of individuals. However, this does not mean that we must also discard the idea of the governmental compact which, in tandem with the force theory, seems able to account satisfactorily for the emergence and perseverance of the modern state. There is little difficulty in accepting the notion that a state may actually originate in the act of a group of people already bound in some form of association, even though we may not be able to formulate an adequate theory of the emergence of that body. Indeed, there are numerous groups of people in existence at this moment who aspire to transform their association into a state with sovereign political authority. Thus, aside from those that arise as the result of conquest or other application of force, one might comfortably suggest that the most likely alternate origin of the state is in a sense of mutuality of interest among a group of people who, as John Austin put it, "were desirous of escaping to a state of government, from a state of anarchy."[1]

The existence of mutual interests among people living in proximity to one another is quite natural and probably inevitable. One may assume that the traditional modes of individual and social conduct found in rudimentary societies are generally sufficient to provide the basis for reasonably stable and tolerable relations between their members, who remain essentially at liberty to pursue their individual interests as they see fit. However, even within the context of a primitive egalitarian society, freedom, as discussed earlier, has both positive and negative aspects. It is positive to the extent that it provides for the right of the individual to self-determined freedom of action; but it is also negative in that it calls upon the individual to impose voluntary self-restraint on the exercise of that freedom in order that he not interfere with the identical freedom of action of others. Thus, Paul Weiss observes: "A society offers people a greater degree of guidance, protection, and success than they themselves separately, or as just together, could provide. Were it not that it has no well-focused or well-controlled power or boundaries, and no stated, intelligible, stable rules and regulations, there would be little need to go beyond it to find other ways to help and protect people who collaborate and associate, sometimes quite well for a time. The help and protection are provided by a state. A state imposes articulated, enforceable demands on people who are together in a society."[2] The power of the state is applied to restraining the actions of individuals insofar as they might interfere with the positive liberty of others within the society. Civil liberty, conceived as a sphere of activity in which the individual is protected from outside interference by some power other than his own physical strength, is possible only in a politically organized society. Accordingly, the existence of the state would clearly seem to be in the interest of each individual and may justifiably be said to rest upon the collectively, although perhaps implicitly, expressed consent of the people.

Nonetheless, in some instances mutuality of interest alone is probably not a sufficiently powerful motivating force and may require supplementation by an inchoate sentiment of community before the state, as its public expression, can come into existence on the basis of the subordination of the communal group to its authority. Salvador de Madariaga wrote: "What is a State? It is a complex of institutions more or less harmoniously connected in theory and in practice, more or less stable, which embodies the collective traditions and administers the collective interests gathered in the course of history by a group of men on a given territory, when, for reasons also historical and involving therefore an element of chance, there exists between them a minimum of solidarity."[3] This is to say that before the state can come into being, the sense of communal solidarity must take such strong hold in the popular consciousness that the people are conditioned to submit to a central ruling authority, surrendering such autonomy of action as they may possess. This does not suggest that prior to that time the people lived in some sort of state of nature, but rather that such societal arrangements as did exist proved ineffective in providing the minimum necessary or desired security of person and property, or did not satisfy some other deeply felt need.

The sentiment for communal solidarity, as suggested by Madariaga, "in which may be discerned animal elements of consanguinity, geographical and climatic elements, sociological elements grown of habit, emotional elements due in part to common remembrances, intellectual elements in which a strong proportion of self-suggestion may be observed—is the root of the feeling of nationality."[4] The sense of nationality also tends to incorporate an inclination toward a community's political autonomy. In this regard, John Stuart Mill wrote: "A portion of mankind may be said to constitute a nationality if they are united among themselves by common sympathies which do not exist between them and any others— which make them co-operate with each other more willingly than with other people, desire to be under the same government, and desire that it should be government by themselves or a portion of themselves exclusively."[5] Mill's suggestion is corroborated by experience, which indicates that it is in fact a common tendency for a group possessed by a feeling of nationality to seek to give it political expression in a state.

The relationship between the nation and the state is often misunderstood, presumably because the sentiments that underlie both are similar in most respects. The conditions that tend to generate feelings of nationality most often are the same as those that urge the formation of the state. Nonetheless, it is appropriate to bear in mind that the two sentiments are not identical, especially where a multinational population is involved. There are groups with a well-developed sense of nationality that have not evinced any strong interest in political unification, and there are instances where groups of people without strong feelings of communal solidarity nonetheless demand the establishment of a state. Indeed, history provides numerous examples of states being formed out of groups of peoples who share few of the elements that contribute to the sentiment of nationality. The sense of nationality may derive from common ethnicity, language, religion, culture, historical circumstance, and other factors that serve to link people together. On the other hand, the demand for the establishment of common political control over a particular territory or community may reflect nothing more than a sense of political expediency, something that is not a factor contributing to the sentiment of nationality. The demand for a state may result simply from an obvious need for the security that a central political authority may offer, perhaps in preventing intercommunal strife.

However, it is not enough that there be a desire, articulated or inchoate, to transform the group into a cohesive body politic in order for the state to emerge. Objective factors may preclude this from happening, temporarily or indefinitely. In our own times, there are numerous examples of peoples wishing to constitute themselves as states who have been prevented from realizing this goal for a variety of reasons. Thus, it is only when the desire for giving a political form to the community results in the establishment of an actual institutional framework for concentrating authority and coercive power over a given people and territory that a state comes into existence. Governments-in-exile, national liberation movements, and other similar organizations do not constitute states, regardless of their assertions to the contrary, until they actually obtain the essential tangible attributes of a state.

Notwithstanding the popularity of the governmental compact theory, with its inherent doctrine of the responsibility of the governors to the governed, the corollary idea that the state is but an instrument for achieving the well-being of its citizens remains problematic. The latter notion of the state as an instrument or mechanism, while quite appealing, seems to be at odds with the evidence of human experience. In this regard, some elements of the organic theory may usefully be applied to consent theory as a corrective to its excesses.

Upon reflection it seems reasonably evident that the state is indeed more of an organism than a mechanism, although by no means a natural organism. The state does bear some close analogies with the human organism. It certainly appears to reflect a will of its own, and to have ends that often transcend the aggregate interests of its living members. The autonomous state tends to exhibit an interest in the future that is sometimes out of step with the mainstream of the society, but it pursues its perception of such interests undeterred. The state, of course, remains an abstraction—it is manifested in reality through the men and institutions that constitute its government. Nonetheless, as discussed in Chapter 5, the state clearly exerts a great influence on the attitudes of those who wear the mantle of its authority. It is not an uncommon experience that persons who opposed the policy directions of the state, when they were outside the framework of government, adopt a rather different attitude when given responsibility for the fate of the state. It would seem that they become subject to the vital interests of the state as if it were a transcendent entity whose continued well-being demands the subordination of other concerns. In a country like the United States, it is not at all unusual to see people who are basically liberal in their political outlook adopt highly conservative positions when faced with the need to secure the long-term interests of the state, even when such is done at the expense of the short-term needs of the people. It thus seems eminently reasonable to consider the state as an artificial creation of man that, once brought into being, becomes a vital organism with ends of its own, and attributes that compare in some respects with those possessed by the people as individuals. And, just as an individual human being who does not exhibit adequate concern for the well-being of its component elements will suffer illness, decay, and accelerated demise, so too with the state. However, we should not press the analogies too far because, in the last analysis, the state is not really a natural organism in any strict sense, even though it exhibits some of the characteristics of one. The key point is that the state is not merely a mechanism for achieving certain fixed purposes. If there is a political entity that possesses the latter characteristic, at least in theory, it is government, as distinct from the state that it manifests and as whose instrument it serves.

The element of organic theory that probably most merits retention is that which attributes personality to the state. Although we may reject the notion of the state as a true organism, it may nonetheless usefully be described as having juridical personality, a quality that we have long assigned to corporations. It seems reasonable to consider the state as a person because it evidently manifests a will of its own, and is generally recognized as having personality in the national consciousness. This concept was elucidated in the last century by Georg Jellinek, who argued that the personality of the state should not be understood as a mere figure of speech. It should be considered a person in the same sense that any other phenomenon is so characterized. After all, a person, as such, is itself an abstraction rather than a concrete being. In other words, personality does not equate to mere physical individuality. The attribution of personality refers to a capacity for unified, continuous, and reasoned exercise of the will. It is unity of purpose, Jellinek insists, that is the principal factor in individuality, that provides a criterion for distinguishing between persons. Without unity of purpose, the individual is only a bundle of natural organisms, a complex of molecules, but certainly not a person.[6] Indeed, when a human being is incapacitated in a manner that affects his unity of purpose, his ability to coherently and cohesively exercise his will, the attribution of legal personality is effectively withdrawn and assigned to another who is deemed competent to act on his behalf. In the strictly juridical (and not in the moral) sense, there can be human beings who are not at the same time considered persons. From this standpoint, the individual is a person only because he is deemed to possess legal rights; he does not have legal rights because he is a person.

Similarly, it is the unity of political purpose that justifies assigning the attribute of personality to the state. Indeed, in some systems of public law the state appears as an entity endowed with legal rights and duties analogous to those held by individuals. It is as such a juristic person that the state is distinguished from the aggregate of citizens who constitute its membership, and without whom it could neither be brought into being nor exist. The state is therefore something more than the mere sum of its parts, just as the human being is more than the sum of its organs. It is on this consideration that the notion of an original social contract founders completely. The state cannot emerge from a contract among individuals because one cannot create a public person from a combination of individual persons. This point was made clear by Bluntschli: "From individuals as such, only an individual development can be obtained. Only private interests and relations can be grounded on private individuals. A sum of individuals never is and never can be a unit, any more than a heap of sand can become a statue. If only the individual spirit and will existed and worked in the individual, the existence of the state as a collective body which lives and is determined by a common spirit and a unified collective will would be inconceivable."[7]

The "true" origin of the state and political authority continues to remain a mystery, and political theorists will persist in their search for a general concept that will provide a satisfactory explanation of the phenomenon of the state. As suggested at the outset of this study, concern with the question of the genesis of the state and its power tends to become a matter of more than theoretical importance as dissatisfaction with prevailing political conditions becomes prominent. While the issue of the legitimacy of the state (as opposed to that of the actions of governments) is not an urgent one in the Western world at this time, there is every indication that it will remain a matter of significant concern in the third world for a long time to come. Since all our lives are affected by what takes place in distant as well as not so distant lands to an extent unprecedented in previous history, the problem of the state is one that merits serious ongoing examination.

Notes

Chapter 1

1. Plato, *The Republic*, 369b-c.
2. For different perspectives on this question, see Alban Dewes Winspear, *The Genesis of Plato's Thought* (New York: S.A. Russell, 1940), pp. 195–202, and R. C. Cross and A. D. Woozley, *Plato's Republic: A Philosophical Commentary* (London: Macmillan, 1960), pp. 75–93. It should be noted that in *The Laws*, 677–681, Plato gives an entirely different account of the origin of the state.
3. David Easton, *A Framework for Political Analysis*, p. 80.
4. Easton, *A Systems Analysis of Political Life*, pp. 21–24.
5. Franz Oppenheimer, *The State*, pp. 12–13.
6. Carl Schmitt, *The Concept of the Political*, p. 19.
7. Ibid., pp. 25–26.
8. Leslie Lipson, *The Great Issues of Politics*, p. 61.
9. Marsilius of Padua, *The Defender of Peace*, I, ch. IV, 3,4,5.
10. Heinrich von Treitschke, *Politics*, p. 3.
11. Westel W. Willoughby, *An Examination of the Nature of the State*, p. 3.
12. Robert Paul Wolff, *In Defense of Anarchism*, p. 3.
13. Agost Pulszky, *Theory of Law and Civil Society*, p. 216.
14. Max Weber, *From Max Weber*, pp. 77–78.

15. Lipson, *The Great Issues of Politics*, p. 72.

16. Joseph R. Strayer, *On the Medieval Origins of the Modern State*, pp. 5–9.

17. Randolph Bourne, "Herd Impulses and the State," in Waldo R. Browne, *Leviathan in Crisis*, p. 100.

18. Benedetto Croce, *Politics and Morals*, pp. 7–8.

19. Johann K. Bluntschli, *The Theory of the State*, p. 15.

20. John W. Burgess, *The Foundations of Political Science*, pp. 53–54.

21. Willoughby, *Nature of the State*, p. 17.

22. Ibid., p. 14.

23. Walter Lippmann, *A Preface to Morals*, pp. 80–81.

Chapter 2

1. Robert H. Lowie, *The Origin of the State*, pp. 2–3. See also Lawrence Krader, *Formation of the State*.

2. Karl Wittfogel, *Oriental Despotism*, p. 18.

3. Cited by Elbert D. Thomas, *Chinese Political Thought*, p. 55.

4. Although historical and geographical factors in ancient Greece led to the development of city-states, rather than a unified state predicated on a broader territorial and population base, there is no sound reason to doubt that the *polis* was a state in every fundamental respect.

5. T. A. Sinclair, *A History of Greek Political Thought*, pp. 16–19. See also Paul Friedländer, *Plato: An Introduction*, pp. 10–11.

6. Heraclitus, Fragments 81–82, in Philip Wheelwright, *Heraclitus*, p. 83.

7. Plato, *Protagoras*, 320–322.

8. Ernest Barker, *Greek Political Theory*, p. 63.

9. Cicero, *On the Commonwealth*, I. 25.

10. Ibid., "Introduction," pp. 51–52.

11. Ibid., I. 26.

12. Ibid.

13. Ibid., I. 32.

14. Tacitus, *Annals*, 3. 26.

15. William Ernest Hocking, *Man and the State*, p. 138.

Chapter 3

1. U.N. Ghoshal, *A History of Indian Political Ideas*, p. 196.

2. Cited by Vishwanath P. Varma, *Studies in Hindu Political Thought and Its Metaphysical Foundations*, p. 239.

3. Ibid., pp. 242–243.

4. Ibid., pp. 244–246.

5. Oscar Cullmann, *The State in the New Testament*, pp. 50–51.

6. Romans 13:1–7. (R. S. V).

7. Matthew 22:21. (R. S. V).

8. Ambrose, *Epist. de basilicis tradendis* 38, t. II.

9. Irenaeus, *Adversus Haereseos* 5. 24. 2.

10. Gerard E. Caspary, *Politics and Exegesis: Origen and the Two Swords*, p. 141.

11. Ibid., p. 151. See also Ernest Barker, *From Alexander to Constantine*, pp. 440–444.

12. Herbert A. Deane, *The Political and Social Ideas of St. Augustine*, pp. 142–146.

13. Muhammad Asad, *The Principles of State and Government in Islam*, p. 39.

14. *The Meaning of the Glorious Koran*, 3:26, p. 64.

15. Cited by Muhammad Asad, *State and Government in Islam*, p. 39.

16. Nizam al-Mulk, *The Book of Government or Rules for Kings*, p. 9.

17. John of Salisbury, *The Statesman's Book*, p. 4.

18. Thomas Aquinas, *On Kingship*, pp. 4–6.

19. Thomas Gilby, *Principality and Polity*, p. xxi.

20. Luther Hess Waring, *The Political Theories of Martin Luther*, p. 79.

21. John Calvin, *On God and Political Duty*, p. 48.

22. Heinrich A. Rommen, *The State in Catholic Thought*, p. 443.

23. Ibid., p. 445.

24. Francisco Suarez, *De Legibus*, III. 1. 4–5.

25. Ibid., III. 2. 3.

26. Nicholas of Cusa, *De Concordantia*, II. xiv. Quoted by Paul E. Sigmund, *Nicholas of Cusa and Medieval Political Thought*, p. 140.

27. Suarez, *De Legibus*, III. 2. 4.

28. Ibid., III. 3. 6.
29. Suarez, *Defensio Fidei*, III. 2. 9.
30. Ibid., III. 2. 17.
31. Suarez, *De Legibus*, II. 4. 6, 8, 11.
32. Charles Issawi, *An Arab Philosophy of History*, p. 101.
33. Ruhollah Khomeini, *Islamic Government*, pp. 17, 19.

Chapter 4

1. *The I Ching*, ch. II.
2. Confucius, *Great Learning*, ch. IX.
3. Leonard Shihlien Hsü, *The Political Philosophy of Confucianism*, p. 35.
4. Cited by Elbert D. Thomas, *Chinese Political Thought*, p. 58.
5. Aristotle, *Politics*, I, 2.
6. Gordon J. Schochet, *Patriarchalism in Political Thought*, pp. 21–24.
7. Jean Bodin, *Six Books of the Commonwealth*, p. 6.
8. Marcus Tullius Cicero, *De Officiis*, I, xvii, 54.
9. Desiderius Erasmus, *The Education of a Christian Prince*, p. 170.
10. Bodin, *Six Books*, pp. 6–7.
11. Quoted by Schochet, *Patriarchalism in Political Thought*, p. 140.
12. Ibid., p. 144.
13. Bolingbroke, Henry St. John, *The Works of Lord Bolingbroke*, IV, p. 194.
14. Henry J. S. Maine, *Ancient Law*, pp. 75–76.
15. Ibid., p. 77.
16. William Samuel Lilly, *First Principles in Politics*, pp. 16–18.
17. Jeremy Bentham, *A Fragment on Government*, note, p. 40.
18. Westel W. Willoughby, *An Examination of the Nature of the State*, pp. 20–21.
19. Edward Jenks, *The State and the Nation*, p. 153.
20. José Ortega y Gasset, *The Revolt of the Masses*, p. 154.
21. Ibid., p. 155.

Chapter 5

1. Johann K. Bluntschli, *The Theory of the State*, p. 300.
2. Adolf Lasson, *System der Rechtsphilosophie*, p. 296.

3. Plato, *The Republic*, 420.

4. Aristotle, *Politics*, I. ii. 12–14, p. 6.

5. Giuseppe Prezzolini, *Machiavelli*, pp. 9–12.

6. Niccolò Machiavelli, *The Discourses*, bk III, ch I.

7. Bluntschli, *The Theory of the State*, p. 64.

8. G.W.F. Hegel, *Hegel's Philosophy of Right*, par. 257, p. 155.

9. Ibid., par. 258 "addition," p. 279.

10. Ibid., par. 269 "addition," p. 282.

11. Jacques Maritain, *Scholasticism and Politics*, pp. 98–100.

12. T. D. Weldon, *States and Morals*, p. 34.

13. Bluntschli, *The Theory of the State*, p. 22.

14. Heinrich von Treitschke, *Politics*, pp. 10–11.

15. Ibid., pp. 11–12.

16. Ernest Barker, *Greek Political Theory*, p. 233.

17. Barker, *Political Thought in England*, pp. 107–108.

18. Bluntschli, *The Theory of the State*, p. 19. See also Heinrich A. Rommen, *The State in Catholic Thought*, ch iv, "The Organic View of the State."

19. Ibid., pp. 19–20.

20. Ibid., p. 22.

21. In Adrian Lyttleton, ed., *Italian Fascisms: From Pareto to Gentile*, pp. 258–260.

22. Ibid., p. 42.

23. Westel W. Willoughby, *The Nature of the State*, p. 38.

Chapter 6

1. Fadhil Zaky Mohamad, *Foundations of Arabic-Islamic Political Thought*, p. 17.

2. Charles Issawi, *An Arab Philosophy of History: Selections from the Prolegomena of Ibn Khaldun of Tunis*, pp. 100–102.

3. Cited by Ann K.S. Lambton, *State and Government in Medieval Islam*, p. 187.

4. Issawi, *Arab Philosophy of History*, p. 103.

5. Ibid., p. 114.

6. Lucy Mair, *Primitive Government*, p. 13.

7. Jean Bodin, *Six Books of the Commonwealth*, pp. 18–19.

8. Quoted in J. A. Fernández-Santamaria, *The State, War and Peace*, p. 24.

9. David Hume, *David Hume's Political Essays*, "Of the Original Contract," p. 47.

10. Ibid., pp. 50–51.

11. Heinrich von Treitschke, *Politics*, p. 16.

12. Thomas E. Holland, *Elements of Jurisprudence*, p. 40.

13. Friedrich Nietzsche, *Genealogy of Morals*, Second Essay, 17, in *The Philosophy of Nietzsche*, pp. 703–704.

14. Franz Oppenheimer, *The State*, p. 8.

15. Frederick Engels, *The Origin of the Family, Private Property, and the State*, pp. 77–78.

16. Ibid., p. 79.

17. Ibid., p. 86.

18. Ibid., p. 88.

19. Ibid., pp. 96–97.

20. Ibid., p. 155.

21. Ibid., pp. 156–157.

22. Ibid., p. 158.

23. Engels, *Anti-Dühring*, p. 385.

24. Vladimir I. Lenin, *State and Revolution*, pp. 8–9.

25. Robert M. MacIver, *The Modern State*, pp. 49–50.

26. William Samuel Lilly, *First Principles in Politics*, p. 19.

27. Rousseau, Jean-Jacques. *The Social Contract*, bk. I, ch. III, pp. 6–7.

28. Benedetto Croce, *Politics and Morals*, pp. 12–13.

29. Ibid.

Chapter 7

1. Charles Maurras, *Mes Idées Politiques* (Paris: Fayard, 1937), in J. S. McClelland, ed., *The French Right: From De Maistre to Maurras*, pp. 274–277.

2. Ernest Barker, *Essays on Government*, pp. 90–91.

3 Plato, *Republic*, 358e–359a.

4. Kautilya, *Arthasastra*, I, 13, pp. 22–23.

5. *Dialogues of the Buddha*, III, p. 88. See discussion in Vishwanath P. Varma, *Studies in Hindu Political Thought and Its Metaphysical Foundations*, pp. 174–185.

6. U.N. Ghoshal, *A History of Indian Political Ideas*, p. 64.

7. Fadhil Zaky Mohamad, *Foundations of Arabic-Islamic Political Thought*, pp. 15–16.

8. James Sullivan, "The Antecedents of the Declaration of Independence," pp. 76–77.

9. J. W. Gough, *The Social Contract*, p. 30.

10. Henry J.S. Maine, *Ancient Law*, pp. 214–215.

11. Nicholas of Cusa, *De Concordantia Catholica*, bk. 2, ch. 14. Cited in Ewart Lewis, *Medieval Political Ideas*, p. 192.

12. Quoted by John Locke, *Two Treatises of Civil Government*, bk. II, ch. XVIII, #200, p. 219.

13. Bolingbroke, Henry St. John, *The Idea of a Patriot King*, p. 30.

14. For an examination and analysis of Bolingbroke's position on the origins of political society, see Isaac Kramnick, "An Augustan Reply to Locke: Bolingbroke on Natural Law and the Origin of Government," *Political Science Quarterly*, vol. 82, no. 4 (December 1967), pp. 571–94.

15. Richard Hooker, *Of the Laws of Ecclesiastical Polity*, bk.I, sect. X, [1] and [4], pp. 188, 190.

16. John Milton, "The Tenure of Kings and Magistrates."

17. Juan de Mariana, *The King and the Education of the King*, bk. 1, ch. 1, pp. 111–113.

18. Johannes Althusius, *The Politics of Johannes Althusius*, p. 22.

19. Ibid., p. 28.

20. Ibid., p. 61.

21. Ibid., p. 116.

22. *Mo-Tzu*, ch. 11, in *The Ethical and Political Works of Motse*. It should be noted that in chapter 12, Mo Tzu offers an alternate version of the origin of the state: "Of old when God and the spirits established the state and cities and installed rulers, it was . . . to bring safety out of danger and order out of confusion." However, this alternate version does not affect his absolutist position.

23. Ibid.

24. Fung Yu-Lan, *A Short History of Chinese Philosophy*, p. 59.

25. Hugo Grotius, *The Law of War and Peace*, bk 1, ch 3, sect. 8.

26. Jean-Jacques Rousseau, *The Social Contract*, bk. I, ch. IV, pp. 8–9.

27. Nakae Chomin, *A Discourse by Three Drunkards on Government*, pp. 64, 66.

Chapter 8

1. Thomas Hobbes, *Leviathan*, ch. XIII, pp. 103, 105.

2. Ibid., ch. XIV, pp. 107–108.

3. Ibid., ch. XVIII, pp. 144–145.

4. Ibid., ch. XXI, p. 187.

5. Ibid., ch. XX, p. 167.

6. Benedict de Spinoza, *A Political Treatise*, ch. I, sect. 7, p. 290.

7. Spinoza, *A Theological-Political Treatise*, ch. V, p. 73.

8. Ibid., pp. 73–74.

9. William Samuel Lilly, *First Principles in Politics*, p. 29.

10. Fred M. Taylor, *The Right of the State to Be*, p. 95.

11. Spinoza, *A Theological-Political Treatise*, ch. XX, p. 259.

12. Spinoza, *Political Treatise*, ch. III, sect. 4, sect. 5, p. 302.

13. Ibid., ch. III, sect. 6, p. 303.

14. Ibid., ch. IV, sect. 4, p. 311.

15. Spinoza, *Philosophy of Benedict de Spinoza*, Letter L, p. 374.

16. Hobbes, *De Cive or The Citizen*, ch. III, p. 56.

17. Hobbes, *Leviathan*, ch. XXVI, p. 226.

18. Ibid., p. 228.

19. John Locke, *Two Treatises of Civil Government,* ch. II, #6, p. 119.

20. Ibid., #13, p. 123.

21. Ibid., ch. VII, #89, p. 160.

22. Ibid., ch. IX, #131, pp. 181–182.

23. Ibid., ch. XIX, #222, pp. 228–229.

24. Ibid., p. 229.

25. Jean-Jacques Rousseau, *The Social Contract*, bk. I, ch. IV, p. 7.

26. Ibid., bk. I, ch. VI, pp. 13–14.

27. Ibid., p. 15.

28. Ibid., bk. III, ch. I, p. 55.

29. Ibid., bk. II, ch. I, p. 23.

30. Ibid., bk. II, ch. IV, p. 28.

31. Ibid., bk. II, ch. III, p. 26.

32. Ibid., bk. I, ch. VII, p. 18.

33. Ibid., bk. IV, ch. II, p. 106.

34. Ibid., bk. III, ch. I, p. 55.

35. Ibid., bk. III, ch. XIV, p. 92.

36. Leonard Krieger, *The Politics of Discretion*, p. 126.

37. Samuel Pufendorf, *De jure naturae* (Frankfurt, 1744), II, 133–134, cited by Krieger, *Politics of Discretion,* p. 122.

38. Pufendorf, *De officio*, II, 107, cited by Krieger, *Politics of Discretion,* p. 123.

Chapter 9

1. Thomas H. Huxley, "Natural and Political Rights," *Essays*, vol. I, p. 349.
2. Bendict de Spinoza, *A Theologico-Political Treatise*, ch. XVI, pp. 200–201.
3. Huxley, *Essays*, p. 351.
4. Thomas Hill Green, *Lectures on the Principles of Political Obligation*, p. 48. According to Thomas E. Holland (*Elements of Jurisprudence*, p. 72): a legal right is "a capacity residing in one man of controlling with the assent and assistance of the State the actions of others."
5. David Hume, "Of the Original Contract," *David Hume's Political Essays*, p. 51.
6. Jean-Jacques Rousseau, *The Social Contract*, bk. II, ch. V, p. 32.
7. Westel W. Willoughby, *The Nature of the State*, p. 126.
8. Paul Weiss, *Toward a Perfected State*, p. 160.
9. Henry J. S. Maine, *Ancient Law*, p. 99.
10. Edmund Burke, *The Philosophy of Edmund Burke*, p. 58.
11. Quoted in Gordon J. Schochet, *Patriarchalism in Political Thought*, p. 125.
12. Ibid., p. 126.
13. Green, *Principles of Political Obligation*, p. 71.

Chapter 10

1. John Austin, *The Province of Jurisprudence Determined*, p. 301.
2. Paul Weiss, *Toward a Perfected State*, p. 170.
3. Salvador de Madariaga, *Anarchy or Hierarchy*, p. 81.
4. Ibid.
5. John Stuart Mill, *Representative Government*, ch. XVI, p. 485.
6. Georg Jellinek, *Gesetz und Verordnung*, p. 192.
7. Johann K. Bluntschli, *Geschichte der neuren Staatswissenschaft*, p. 348.

Bibliography

Althusius, Johannes. *The Politics of Johannes Althusius*. Boston: Beacon Press, 1964.

Aquinas, Thomas. *On Kingship: To the King of Cyprus*. Trans. by Gerald B. Phelan, rev. by I. Th. Eschmann. Toronto: Pontifical Institute of Medieval Studies, 1949.

Aristotle. *The Politics of Aristotle*. Ed. by Ernest Barker. New York: Oxford University Press, 1962.

Asad, Muhammad. *The Principles of State and Government in Islam*. Berkeley and Los Angeles: University of California Press, 1961

Augustine. *The Political Writings of St. Augustine*. Ed. by Henry Paolucci. Chicago: Henry Regnery, 1962.

Austin, John. *The Province of Jurisprudence Determined*. London: Weidenfeld and Nicolson, 1954.

Barker, Ernest. *Essays on Government*. 2nd ed. Oxford: Clarendon Press, 1951.

————. *From Alexander to Constantine: Passages and Documents Illustrating the History of Social and Political Ideas, 336 B.C.– A.D. 337*. Oxford: Clarendon Press, 1956.

————. *Greek Political Theory: Plato and His Predecessors*. New York: Barnes & Noble, 1957.

————. *Political Thought in England: From Herbert Spencer to the Present Day*. New York: Henry Holt, n.d.

————. *The Political Thought of Plato and Aristotle*. New York: Dover Publications, 1959.

Becker, Howard and Leon Smelo. "Conflict Theories of the State," *The Sociological Review,*. Vol. 23, no. 2 (July 1931), pp. 65–79.

Bellarmine, Robert. *De Laicis or The Treatise On Civil Government*. Trans. by Kathleen E. Murphy. New York: Fordham University Press, 1928.

Bentham, Jeremy. *A Fragment on Government and An Introduction to the Principles of Morals and Legislation*. Oxford: Basil Blackwell, 1948.

Bluntschli, Johann K. *Geschichte der neuren Staatswissenschaft*. Munich and Leipzig: R. Oldenbourg, 1881.

————. *The Theory of the State*. 2nd ed. Oxford: Clarendon Press, 1895.

Bodin, Jean. *Six Books of the Commonwealth*. Abr. and trans. by M. J. Tooley. Oxford: Basil Blackwell, n.d.

Bolingbroke, Henry St John. *The Idea of a Patriot King*. Indianapolis: Library of Liberal Arts, 1965.

———— *The Works of Lord Bolingbroke*. 4 vols. Philadelphia: Carey and Hart, 1841.

Browne, Waldo R., ed. *Leviathan in Crisis*. New York: Viking Press, 1946.

Burgess, John W. *The Foundations of Political Science*. New York: Columbia University Press, 1933.

Burke, Edmund. *The Philosophy of Edmund Burke*. Ed. by Louis I. Brevold and Ralph G. Ross. Ann Arbor: University of Michigan Press, 1960.

Calvin, John. *On God and Political Duty*. Ed. by John T. McNeill. Indianapolis: Library of Liberal Arts, 1956.

Caspary, Gerard E. *Politics and Exegesis: Origen and the Two Swords*. Berkeley: University of California Press, 1979.

Cicero, Marcus Tullius. *De Officiis*. Trans. by Walter Miller. London: Loeb Classical Library, 1913.

————. *On the Commonwealth*. Trans. with notes and intro. by George H. Sabine and Stanley B. Smith. Columbus: Ohio State University Press, 1929.

Confucius. *Great Learning*. In James Legge, *The Chinese Classics*. 2nd ed. Vol. I. Oxford: Clarendon Press, 1893.

Croce, Benedetto. *Politics and Morals*. New York: Philosophical Library, 1945.

Cullmann, Oscar. *The State in the New Testament*. New York: Scribner's, 1956.

Daly, L.J. *The Political Theory of John Wyclif.* Chicago: Loyola University Press, 1962.

Dante. *Monarchy and Three Political Letters.* Trans. with an intro. by Donald Nicholl. New York: Noonday Press, n.d.

Deane, Herbert A. *The Political and Social Ideas of St. Augustine.* New York: Columbia University Press, 1963.

De Grazia, Sebastian. *Masters of Chinese Political Thought: From the Beginnings to the Han Dynasty.* New York: Viking Press, 1973

De Jassy, Anthony. *The State.* Oxford: Basil Blackwell, 1985.

Dialogues of the Buddha. Trans. by T. W. Rhys Davids. Vol. III. London: Oxford University Press, 1921.

Easton, David. *A Framework for Political Analysis.* Englewood Cliffs, N.J.: Prentice-Hall, 1965.

————. *A Systems Analysis of Political Life.* New York: John Wiley & Sons, 1965.

Engels, Frederick. *Anti-Dühring.* 3rd ed. Moscow: Foreign Languages Publishing House, 1962.

————. *The Origin of the Family, Private Property, and the State.* New York: International Publishers, 1942.

Erasmus, Desiderius. *The Education of a Christian Prince.* Ed. and trans. by Lester K. Born. New York: Columbia University Press, 1936.

Fernández-Santamaria, J. A. *The State, War and Peace: Spanish Political Thought in the Renaissance 1516–1559.* Cambridge: Cambridge University Press, 1977.

Friedländer, Paul. *Plato: An Introduction.* New York: Harper & Row, 1964.

Fung Yu-Lan. *A Short History of Chinese Philosophy.* New York: Macmillan, 1964.

Geisst, Charles R. *The Political Thought of John Milton.* London: Macmillan, 1984.

Ghoshal, U.N. *A History of Indian Political Ideas.* London: Oxford University Press, 1966.

Gilby, Thomas. *Principality and Polity: Aquinas and the Rise of State Theory in the West.* London: Longmans, Green, 1958.

Gough, J. W. *The Social Contract: A Critical Study of its Development.* Westport, Conn.: Greenwood Press, 1978.

Green, Thomas Hill. *Lectures on the Principles of Political Obligation.* London: Longmans, Green, 1921.

Grotius, Hugo. *The Law of War and Peace.* Trans. by Louise R. Loomis. Roslyn, N.Y.: Walter J. Black, 1949.

Hamilton, Bernice. *Political Thought in Sixteenth-Century Spain*. Oxford: Clarendon Press, 1963.

Hegel, G.W.F. *Hegel's Philosophy of Right*. Trans. by T. M. Knox. London: Oxford University Press, 1967.

———. *Hegel's Political Writings*. Trans. by T. M. Knox, with intro. by Z.A. Pelczynski. Oxford: Clarendon Press, 1964.

Hobbes, Thomas. *De Cive or The Citizen*. New York: Appleton-Century-Crofts, 1949.

———. *Leviathan*. New York: E.P. Dutton, 1950.

Hocking, William Ernest. *Man and the State*. New Haven: Yale University Press, 1926.

Holland, Thomas E. *Elements of Jurisprudence*. 6th ed. Oxford: Clarendon Press, 1893.

Hooker, Richard. *Of the Laws of Ecclesiastical Polity*. Vol. I. London: J.M. Dent, n.d.

Hsü, Leonard Shihlien. *The Political Philosophy of Confucianism*. New York: E.P. Dutton, 1932.

Hume, David. *David Hume's Political Essays*. Ed. by Charles W. Hendel. New York: Liberal Arts Press, 1953.

Huxley, Thomas H. *Essays*. Vol. 1. Westport, Conn.: Greenwood Press, 1968.

The I Ching. Trans. by James Legge. 2nd ed. Oxford: Clarendon Press, 1899.

Issawi, Charles. *An Arab Philosophy of History: Selections from the Prolegomena of Ibn Khaldun of Tunis*. London: John Murray, 1950.

Jellinek, Georg. *Die Lehre von der Staatenverbindungen*. Berlin: O. Haering, 1882.

———. *Gesetz und Verordnung*. Tübingen: J.C.B. Mohr, 1919.

Jenks, Edward. *The State and the Nation*. New York: E.P. Dutton, 1919.

John of Salisbury. *The Statesman's Book of John of Salisbury*. Trans. with Intro by John Dickinson. New York: Russell & Russell, 1963.

Kautilya. *Arthasastra*. Trans. by R. Shamasastry. Mysore: Mysore Printing and Publishing, 1967.

Khomeini, Ruhollah. *Islamic Government*. New York: Manor Books, 1979.

Krader, Lawrence. *The Formation of the State*. Englewood Cliffs, N.J.: Prentice-Hall, 1968.

Kramnick, Isaac. "An Augustan Reply to Locke: Bolingbroke on Natural Law and the Origin of Government." *Political Sci-*

ence Quarterly, Vol. 82, no. 4 (December 1967), pp. 571–594.

Krieger, Leonard. *The Politics of Discretion: Pufendorf and the Acceptance of Natural Law*. Chicago: University of Chicago Press, 1965.

Lambton, Ann K.S. *State and Government in Medieval Islam*. New York: Oxford University Press, 1981.

Lasson, Adolf. *System der Rechtsphilosophie*. Berlin: J.Guttentag, 1882.

Lenin, Vladimir I. *State and Revolution*. New York: International Publishers, 1943.

Lewis, Ewart. *Medieval Political Ideas*. Vol. 1. New York: Cooper Square Publishers, 1974.

Lilly, William Samuel. *First Principles in Politics*. New York: G.P. Putnam's Sons, 1899.

Lippmann, Walter. *A Preface to Morals*. New York: Macmillan, 1929.

Lipson, Leslie. *The Great Issues of Politics*. 4th ed. Englewood Cliffs N.J.: Prentice-Hall, 1970.

Locke, John. *Two Treatises of Civil Government*. London: J.M. Dent, 1924.

Lowie, Robert H. *The Origin of the State*. New York: Russell & Russell, 1962.

Lyttleton, Adrian, ed. *Italian Fascisms: From Pareto to Gentile*. New York: Harper & Row, 1975.

McClelland, J. S., ed. *The French Right: From De Maistre to Maurras*. New York: Harper & Row, 1970.

McGrade, Arthur S. *The Political Thought of William of Ockham: Personal and Institutional Principles*. Cambridge: Cambridge University Press, 1974.

Machiavelli, Niccolò. *The Prince and The Discourses*. New York: Modern Library, 1940.

MacIver, Robert M. *The Modern State*. London: Oxford University Press, 1926.

McShea, Robert J. *The Political Philosophy of Spinoza*. New York: Columbia University Press, 1968.

Madariaga, Salvador de. *Anarchy or Hierarchy*. New York: Macmillan, 1937.

Maine, Henry J. S. *Ancient Law*. London: J. M. Dent, 1917.

Mair, Lucy. *Primitive Government*. Baltimore: Penguin Books, 1964.

Mariana, Juan de. *The King and the Education of the King*. Trans.

by George A. Moore. Washington: Country Dollar Press, 1948.

Maritain, Jacques. *Scholasticism and Politics*. Garden City, N.Y.: Image Books, 1960.

Marsilius of Padua. *The Defender of Peace*. Trans, by Alan Gewirth. New York: Columbia University Press, 1956.

The Meaning of the Glorious Koran. Explained and trans. by Mohammed Marmaduke Pickthall. New York: New American Library, 1953.

Mill, John Stuart. *Utilitarianism, Liberty, and Representative Government*. New York: E. P. Dutton, 1951.

Milton, John. "The Tenure of Kings and Magistrates," in *Complete Prose Works of John Milton*. Vol. 3. Edited by Don M. Wolfe. New Haven: Yale University Press, 1962.

Mohamad, Fadhil Zaky. *Foundations of Arabic-Islamic Political Thought*. Baghdad: Ministry of Culture and Guidance, 1964.

Mo Tzu. *The Ethical and Political Works of Motse*. Trans. by Y.P. Mei. London: Probsthain, 1929.

Nakae Chomin. *A Discourse by Three Drunkards on Government*. Trans. by Noboku Tsukui. New York: Weatherhill, 1984.

Nietzsche, Friedrich. *The Philosophy of Nietzsche*. New York: Modern Library, n.d.

Nisbet, Robert A. *Community and Power*. New York: Oxford University Press, 1962.

Nizam al-Mulk. *The Book of Government or Rules for Kings*. Trans. by Hubert Darke. New Haven: Yale University Press, 1960.

Oppenheimer, Franz. *The State*. Montreal: Black Rose Books, 1975.

Ortega y Gasset, José. *The Revolt of the Masses*. New York: W.W. Norton, 1957.

Plato. *The Dialogues of Plato*. Trans. by B. Jowett. 4 vols. Oxford: Clarendon Press, 1953.

Poggi, Gianfranco. *The Development of the Modern State*. Stanford, Cal.: Stanford University Press, 1978.

Prezzolini, Giuseppe. *Machiavelli*. New York: Farrar, Straus & Giroux, 1967.

Pulszky, Agost. *Theory of Law and Civil Society*. London: T.F. Unwin, 1888.

Rommen, Heinrich A. "Francis Suarez," *The Review of Politics*, Vol. 10, no. 4. (October 1948), pp. 437–461.

———. *The State in Catholic Thought.* St. Louis: B. Herder, 1945.

Rosenthal, E. I. J. *Political Thought in Medieval Islam.* Cambridge: Cambridge University Press, 1962.

Rousseau, Jean-Jacques. *The Social Contract and Discourses.* New York: E.P. Dutton, 1950.

Sait, Edward M. *Political Institutions: A Preface.* New York: Appleton-Century, 1938.

Schmitt, Carl. *The Concept of the Political.* Trans. by George Schwab. New Brunswick, N.J.: Rutgers University Press, 1976.

Schochet, Gordon J. *Patriarchalism in Political Thought.* New York: Basic Books, 1975.

Sigmund, Paul E. *Nicholas of Cusa and Medieval Political Thought.* Cambridge, Mass.: Harvard University Press, 1963.

Sinclair, T.A. *A History of Greek Political Thought.* Cleveland: World Publishing, 1968.

Spinoza, Benedict de. *Philosophy of Spinoza.* Includes: *On the Improvement of the Understanding, The Ethics* and *The Correspondence.* New York: Tudor Publishing, n.d.

———. *A Theologico-Political Treatise and A Political Treatise.* New York: Dover, 1951.

Strayer, Joseph R. *On the Medieval Origins of the Modern State.* Princeton, N.J.: Princeton University Press, 1970.

Suarez, Francisco. *Selections from Three Works of Francisco Suarez.* Translated by Gwladys L. Williams, Ammi Brown and John Waldron, Oxford: Clarendon Press, 1944.

Sullivan, James. "The Antecedents of the Declaration of Independence." In the *Annual Report of the American Historical Association* for 1902. Vol. 1, pp. 67–81.

Tacitus. *The Complete Works of Tacitus.* Trans. by Alfred J. Church and William J. Brodribb. New York: Modern Library, 1942.

Taylor, Fred M. *The Right of the State to Be.* Ph. D. Thesis, University of Michigan at Ann Arbor, 1891.

Thomas, Elbert D. *Chinese Political Thought: A Study Based Upon the Theories of the Principal Thinkers of the Chou Period.* New York: Prentice-Hall, 1927.

Treitschke, Heinrich von. *Politics.* Abr. and ed. by Hans Kohn. New York: Harcourt, Brace & World, 1963.

Varma, Vishwanath P. *Studies in Hindu Political Thought and Its Metaphysical Foundations.* 2nd ed. Delhi: Motilal Barnaesidass, 1959.

Waring, Luther Hess. *The Political Theories of Martin Luther*. Port Washington New York: Kennikat Press, 1968.

Watson, John. *The State in Peace and War*. Glasgow: James Maclehose and Sons, 1919.

Weber, Max. *From Max Weber: Essays in Sociology*. Trans. and ed. by H. H. Gerth and C. Wright Mills. New York: Oxford University Press, 1958.

Weiss, Paul. *Toward a Perfected State*. Albany: State University of New York Press, 1986.

Weldon, T. D. *States and Morals: A Study in Political Conflicts*. New York: Whittlesey House, 1947.

Wheelwright, Philip. *Heraclitus*. New York: Atheneum, 1964.

Whelan, Frederick G. "Vattel's Doctrine of the State," *History of Political Thought*. Vol. 9. no. 1. (Spring 1988). pp. 59–90.

Willoughby, Westel W. *An Examination of The Nature of the State: A Study in Political Philosophy*. New York: Macmillan, 1928.

Wittfogel, Karl. *Oriental Despotism*. New Haven: Yale University Press, 1957.

Wolff, Robert Paul. *In Defense of Anarchism*. New York: Harper & Row, 1970.

Index

ABOUT THE AUTHOR

MARTIN SICKER earned his Ph.D. in political science from the graduate faculty of the New School for Social Research in New York. He has served as a senior executive in the U.S. government and has taught political science at The American University and George Washington University in Washington, D.C. He has written widely in the fields of political science and international affairs, and is the author of *The Making of a Pariah State: The Adventurist Politics of Muammar Qaddafi* (Praeger, 1987), *The Judaic State: A Study in Rabbinic Political Theory* (Praeger, 1988), *The Strategy of Soviet Imperialism: Expansion in Eurasia* (Praeger, 1988), *The Bear and the Lion: Soviet Imperialism and Iran* (Praeger, 1988), *Israel's Quest for Security* (Praeger, 1989), and *Between Hashemites and Zionists: The Struggle for Palestine, 1908–1988*.

Dr. Sicker is now a private consultant and lecturer on politics and international affairs. He resides in Silver Springs, Maryland.